THE CONGRESSIONAL BUDGET OFFICE'S BUDGET AND ECONOMIC OUTLOOK

HEARING

BEFORE THE

COMMITTEE ON THE BUDGET
HOUSE OF REPRESENTATIVES

ONE HUNDRED FIFTEENTH CONGRESS

FIRST SESSION

HEARING HELD IN WASHINGTON, DC, FEBRUARY 2, 2017

Serial No. 115–02

Printed for the use of the Committee on the Budget

Available on the Internet:
www.gpo.gov/fdsys/browse/committee.action?chamber=house&committee=budget

U.S. GOVERNMENT PUBLISHING OFFICE

25–238 WASHINGTON : 2017

For sale by the Superintendent of Documents, U.S. Government Publishing Office
Internet: bookstore.gpo.gov Phone: toll free (866) 512–1800; DC area (202) 512–1800
Fax: (202) 512–2104 Mail: Stop IDCC, Washington, DC 20402–0001

COMMITTEE ON THE BUDGET

DIANE BLACK, Tennessee, *Interim Chairman*

TODD ROKITA, Indiana, *Vice Chairman*
MARIO DIAZ-BALART, Florida
TOM COLE, Oklahoma
TOM McCLINTOCK, California
ROB WOODALL, Georgia
MARK SANFORD, South Carolina
STEVE WOMACK, Arkansas
DAVE BRAT, Virginia
GLENN GROTHMAN, Wisconsin
GARY J. PALMER, Alabama
BRUCE WESTERMAN, Arkansas
JAMES B. RENACCI, Ohio
BILL JOHNSON, Ohio
JASON SMITH, Missouri
JASON LEWIS, Minnesota
JACK BERGMAN, Michigan
JOHN J. FASO, New York
LLOYD SMUCKER, Pennsylvania
MATT GAETZ, Florida
JODEY C. ARRINGTON, Texas
A. DREW FERGUSON IV, Georgia

JOHN A. YARMUTH, Kentucky,
Ranking Minority Member
BARBARA LEE, California
MICHELLE LUJAN GRISHAM, New Mexico
SETH MOULTON, Massachusetts
HAKEEM S. JEFFRIES, New York
BRIAN HIGGINS, New York
SUZAN K. DELBENE, Washington
DEBBIE WASSERMAN SCHULTZ, Florida
BRENDAN F. BOYLE, Pennsylvania
RO KHANNA, California
PRAMILA JAYAPAL, Washington
Vice Ranking Minority Member
SALUD O. CARBAJAL, California
SHEILA JACKSON LEE, Texas
JANICE D. SCHAKOWSKY, Illinois

PROFESSIONAL STAFF

RICHARD E. MAY, *Staff Director*
ELLEN BALIS, *Minority Staff Director*

CONTENTS

THE CONGRESSIONAL BUDGET OFFICE'S BUDGET AND ECONOMIC OUTLOOK

THURSDAY, FEBRUARY 2, 2017

HOUSE OF REPRESENTATIVES,
COMMITTEE ON THE BUDGET,
Washington, DC.

The committee met, pursuant to call, at 10:00 a.m., in Room 1334, Longworth House Office Building, Hon. Diane Black [interim chairman of the committee] presiding.

Present: Representatives Black, Cole, McClintock, Sanford, Grothman, Renacci, Johnson, Lewis, Faso, Smucker, Arrington, Ferguson, Yarmuth, Moulton, Jeffries, Higgins, DelBene, Wasserman Schultz, and Khanna.

Interim Chair BLACK. The hearing will come to order. Welcome to the Committee on the Budget Hearing on the Congressional Budget Office's Budget and Outlook. I want to thank everyone for being here this morning. We are holding this hearing today to discuss the Congressional Budget Office's budget and economic outlook which gives us a 10 year projection of our spending, our national debt, and how the economy is going to perform over the next decade.

The report forms the cornerstone of the work we do here at the House Budget Committee, and I want to thank everyone at the CBO for their hard work in producing this report. I would also like to welcome the CBO director, Keith Hall. Director Hall, I do appreciate your taking the time to testify today, and I look forward to your insight as we discuss this report.

The discussion we will have today is a serious one because as CBO indicates, we face enormous fiscal and economic challenges. Deficits are beginning to rise again and economic growth continues to be subpar. Legacies of the last administration's policies that encourage more spending, more debt, and more government. These challenges have a real impact on every person in this country.

The numbers we are reviewing today affect the ability of every American to buy groceries, obtain a loan, to start a small business, or to get a good return on their retirement plan. We know this to be the case because CBO's report is telling us of what would happen if we kept President Obama's policies in place. Without any changes to the current law, the deficit would rise from $587 billion in fiscal year 2016 to $1.4 trillion in fiscal year 2027. And during that same time period, our national debt will jump to $30 trillion.

To put that in human terms, that is $93,000 for every American. And for a lot of folks, that is about what it costs to buy a home.

CBO tells us that this ever-increasing debt spiral will hamper economic growth and consign the country to a lower standard of living

As a grandmother, I want my grandchildren to have every opportunity that I did. But on our current path, the dream of a good job or owning a home and sending their kids to college is becoming harder and harder. Much of this unsustainable fiscal path is driven by projected spending for Medicare, Medicaid, and Social Security over the next decade. But without reforms, these programs are going to fail our seniors who have worked hard and paid into them for their entire lives.

To compound these problems, economic growth is set to average at a morbid 1.9 percent over the coming decade, well below the historic average of just over three percent.

Slow economic growth hurts our country in multiple ways. It means fewer jobs and less opportunities for Americans, it means smaller paychecks and less financial security for those Americans who have a job. In fact, more than 5 million Americans are working part-time because they cannot find a fulltime job.

That means that we got welders, computer technicians, nurses, and people in all sorts of industries who want to contribute to our economy, but they are being let down by the rules and regulations coming out of Washington. The problem is particularly acute among men.

One of the key symptoms of this subpar economic recovery has been the decline in the labor workforce participant rate of those of primary working age. And here is a story from a gentleman named Chris back in my own district in Tennessee.

He said he was laid off just last year, and in his letter, he said this to me, and I want to quote, I worked at this job for 7 years. I am a hard worker and I have never tried for any government assistance. I am positive I will have a job soon, but I have been without a paycheck for months now, and if I have to wait anymore, I will have no money for utilities or support for me, my wife and 7-year-old.

Now, it is pretty clear that Chris is exactly the type of worker that makes our economy the best in the world, and he is a good husband and father who wants to take care of his family. Chris wants to make our country stronger, and it is our job to help give him that opportunity. A job is so much more than the way we pay for rent or put gas in our car. A job helps us to define ourselves. It gives people a sense of purpose. It helps to build communities, and it can break cycles of poverty, and when Americans have a steady job, they know the dignity of work.

CBO's report tells us what will happen if we do nothing, but that is certainly not the only choice we have. We can choose to get our fiscal house back under control. We can choose to get our economy growing again so that it works for men and women of this country. And here, at the House Budget Committee, that is exactly what we intend to do.

Director Hall, thank you again for being here, and I look forward to your testimony in how I can help guide us informing the best policies to hold the Federal Government accountable, grow our economy, and serve the American people. And with that, I yield to my ranking member, Mr. Yarmuth.

[The prepared statement of Interim Chair Black follows:]

BLACK OPENING STATEMENT:

HEARING ON CBO'S BUDGET AND ECONOMIC OUTLOOK

Washington, February 2, 2017

As prepared for delivery – House Budget Committee Interim Chairman Diane Black

Good morning, and thank you, everyone for being here.

We're holding this hearing today to discuss the Congressional Budget Office's Budget and Economic Outlook – which gives us ten-year projections of our spending, national debt, and how the economy is going to perform over the next decade.

The report forms the cornerstone of the work we do here at the House Budget Committee, and I want to thank everyone at CBO for all their hard work in producing this report. I'd also like to welcome CBO Director Keith Hall. Director Hall – I appreciate you taking the time to testify today and I look forward to your insight as we discuss this report.

The discussion we will have today is a serious one, because as CBO indicates, we face enormous fiscal and economic challenges. Deficits are beginning to rise again and economic growth continues to be subpar – legacies of the last administration's policies that encouraged more spending, more debt, and more government. These challenges have a real impact on every person in this country. The numbers we're reviewing today affect the ability of every American to buy groceries, obtain a loan to start a small business, or get a good return on their retirement plan.

We know this to be the case because CBO's report is telling us what would happen if we kept President Obama's policies in place. Without any changes to current law, the deficit would rise from $587 billion in fiscal year 2016 to $1.4 trillion in fiscal year 2027. During that same period, our national debt will jump to $30 trillion. To put that in human terms, that's $93,000 for every American. For a lot of folks, that's about what it costs to buy a home.

CBO tells us that this ever-increasing debt spiral will hamper economic growth and consign the country to a lower standard of living. As a grandmother, I want my grandchildren to have every opportunity I did. But on our current path, the dream of a good job, owning a home, and sending their kids to college is becoming harder and harder.

Much of this unsustainable fiscal path is driven by projected spending for Medicare, Medicaid, and Social Security over the next decade. But without reforms, these programs are going to fail our seniors who have worked hard and paid into them their entire lives.

To compound these problems, economic growth is set to average at a morbid 1.9 percent over the coming decade, well below the historic average of just over 3 percent. Slow economic growth hurts our country in multiple ways – it means fewer jobs and less opportunity for Americans, and it means smaller paychecks and less financial security for those Americans who do have a job. In fact, more than 5 million Americans are working part-time because they can't find a full-time job. That means we've got welders, computer technicians, nurses, and people in all sorts of industries who want to contribute to our economy, but they're being let down by the rules and regulations coming out of Washington.

The problem is particularly acute among men. One of the key symptoms of this subpar economic recovery has been the decline in the labor force participation rate of those in their prime working age. And here's a story from a gentleman named Chris back in my district in Tennessee. He said he was laid off last year, and in his letter to me he said, "I worked at this job for 7 years and I'm a hard worker and have never tried for any government assistance. I'm positive I'll have a job soon but I've been without a paycheck for months now. If I have to wait any more I will have no money for utilities or to support me, my wife, and 7 year old."

Now it's pretty clear that Chris is exactly the type of worker that makes our economy the best in the world, and he's a good husband and father who just wants to take care of his family. Chris wants to make our country stronger, and it's our job to help give him that opportunity.

A job is so much more than a way to pay for rent and put gas in the car. A job helps us define ourselves. It gives people a sense of purpose, helps build strong communities, and can break cycles of poverty. When Americans have a steady job, they know the dignity of work.

CBO's report tells us what will happen if we do nothing, but that is certainly not the only choice we have. We can choose to get our fiscal house back under control. And we can choose to get our economy growing again so that it works for the men and women of this country. And here at the House Budget Committee, that is exactly what we intend to do.

Director Hall – again, thank you for being here. I look forward to your testimony and how it can help guide us in forming the best policies to hold the federal government accountable, grow the economy, and serve the American people.

With that, I yield to the ranking member, Mr. Yarmuth.

Mr. YARMUTH. Thank you, Chairman Black, and thank you, Director Hall for appearing before us today to outline CBO's updated economic and budget outlook. Long-term outlook remains troubling, of course. We are a few years away from an increase in Federal deficits and debt driven by the increased healthcare and retirement costs of an older population.

Your report outlines our circumstances as a new administration takes office. Total deficits over 10 years are essentially the same as you projected in August. You projected this year's deficit to be lower than last year's and next year's to be lower still, and as your report says, the economy is currently on solid ground. That is a much better starting point than President Obama faced 8 years ago. President Obama inherited an economy in freefall. The country was in the midst of the deepest recession in generations, losing nearly 800,000 jobs per month.

In its January 2009 outlook, CBO was projecting a deficit of more than $1 trillion and the economy was projected to shrink by 2.2 percent. That turned out to be optimistic. In contrast, President Trump is inheriting a healthy economy.

The economy has added 15.8 million private sector jobs since 2010. The unemployment rate is less than half its 2009 peak, and the budget deficit has fallen by more than $800 billion, a nearly two-thirds reduction as a share of the economy. This year's CBO report projects that the economy will grow at a 2.3 percent rate. Job creation will also grow at a steady rate, and the deficit will shrink over the next 2 years. What a difference 8 years makes. President Obama's economic agenda is also paying dividends on many other fronts. Tens of millions of Americans now have the economic security that comes with having health coverage and thereby being free from fears of an accident or illness sending them into bankruptcy. Stock market has tripled in value, the auto industry has recovered from a near death experience, manufacturing has added jobs for the first time since the 1990s, and wages have begun to grow at a healthy pace.

The financial industry is better capitalized and more secure with stronger protections for consumers. We have dramatically reduced our dependence on foreign oil and increased our production of renewable energy. Housing prices have largely recovered and millions of home owners are no longer under water on their mortgages. I could go on and on, and I probably should because I know my colleagues on the other side of the aisle will present an alternative reality.

I am dealing in facts, and the fact is this Congress and the new Trump administration are getting ready to take our country down a far different path. Republican leadership is moving to repeal the Affordable Care Act with no plan to replace it. Thirty-two million people will lose health coverage, premiums will double, and we will return to the days when insurance companies decide who lives and who dies. House Republicans are planning deep tax cuts and a rollback of financial protections. Recent Republican Presidents have tried this approach.

Each time, it resulted in skyrocketing deficits, a recession, and ultimately a financial crisis, the most recent of which brought our country to the brink of total collapse. I was briefed by Paulson and

Bernanke in 2008. I know how close our Nation came to having the lights go out. The American people cannot afford for us to make those same mistakes again.

Finally, I want to raise the issue of immigration. It has been heart wrenching to see the immediate impact of the President's executive order during the past week. It is discouraging that the first immigration action of this White House separated families, vilified the innocent, and will fail to make our Nation safer by every logical measure.

That being said, I was a member of the Gang of Eight in 2013, four democrats and four republicans. We drafted comprehensive immigration reform legislation that we were confident had the bipartisan votes to pass the house. The only thing missing was the political will of Republican leadership to bring it to the floor.

Beyond addressing humanitarian and security needs, CBO has repeatedly told us that comprehensive immigration reform would mean a larger economy and a smaller budget deficit. It is my hope that my colleagues across the aisle will recognize these facts and enact the immigration reform we so desperately need. We cannot solve the challenges we face as a Nation whether it is immigration, health care, the economy, or passing a congressional budget without acknowledging what got us here and continuing on that path.

To return to where we were and abandon all the progress we have made would be devastating, not just for American families today but for generations to come. With that, Director Hall, I look forward to your testimony. I yield back.

[The prepared statement of Mr. Yarmuth follows:]

YARMUTH WARNS GOP NOT TO TURN BACK THE CLOCK ON PROGRESS IN CBO HEARING

February 2, 2017

Washington, D.C. — Today, Kentucky Congressman John Yarmuth, Ranking Member of the House Budget Committee, highlighted the importance of protecting the economic and health care gains made under President Obama at a hearing titled "The Congressional Budget Office's Budget and Economic Outlook" with CBO Director Keith Hall. Yarmuth spoke out against the negative consequences of House Republican efforts to repeal the Affordable Care Act, pass un-funded tax breaks for the rich, and block immigrants and refugees from entering our country.

Thank you, Chairman Black. And thank you Director Hall for appearing before us today to outline CBO's updated economic and budget outlook.

The long-term outlook remains troubling of course. We are a few years away from an increase in federal deficits and debt driven by the increased health care and retirement costs of an older population.

Your report outlines our circumstances as a new Administration takes office. Total deficits over ten years are essentially the same as you projected in August. You project this year's deficit to be lower than last year's. And next year's to be lower still. And as your report says, "the economy is currently on solid ground."

That's a much better starting point than President Obama faced eight years ago. President Obama inherited an economy in free fall. The country was in the midst of the deepest recession in generations, losing nearly 800,000 jobs per month. In its January 2009 outlook, CBO was projecting a deficit of more than $1 trillion and the economy was projected to shrink by 2.2 percent. That turned out to be optimistic.

In contrast, President Trump is inheriting a healthy economy. The economy has added 15.8 million private sector jobs since 2010. The unemployment rate is less than half its 2009 peak and the budget deficit has fallen by more than $800 billion, a nearly two-thirds reduction as a share of the economy.

This year's CBO report projects that the economy will grow at a 2.3 percent rate. Job creation will also grow at a steady rate, and the deficit will shrink over the next two years.

What a difference eight years makes.

President Obama's economic agenda is also paying dividends on many other fronts. Tens of millions of Americans now have the economic security that comes with having health coverage and are free from fears of an accident or illness sending them into bankruptcy.

The stock market has nearly tripled in value. The auto industry has recovered from a near-death experience, manufacturing has added jobs for the first time since the 1990s, and wages have begun to grow at a healthy pace. The financial industry is better capitalized and more secure, with stronger protections for consumers. We have dramatically reduced our dependence on foreign oil and increased our production of renewable energy. Housing prices have largely recovered, and millions of homeowners are no longer underwater on their mortgages.

I could go on and on and I should, because I know my colleagues on the other side of the aisle will present an alternative reality.

I am dealing in facts. And the fact is this Congress and the new Trump Administration are getting ready to take our country down a far different path.

Republican Leadership is moving to repeal the Affordable Care Act with no plan to replace it. 32 million people will lose health coverage, premiums will double, and we will return to the days when insurance companies decide who lives and who dies.

House Republicans are planning deep tax cuts and a rollback of financial protections. Recent Republican Presidents have tried this approach. Each time, it resulted in skyrocketing deficits, a recession, and ultimately a financial crisis, the most recent of which brought our country to the brink of total collapse. I was briefed by Paulson and Bernanke in 2008. I know how close our nation came to having the lights go out. The American people cannot afford for us to make those same mistakes again.

Finally, I want to raise the issue of immigration. It has been heart-wrenching to see the immediate impact of the President's Executive Order during the past week. It is discouraging that the first immigration action of this White House separated families, vilified the innocent, and will fail to make our nation safer by every logical measure.

That being said, I was a member of the Gang of 8 in 2013. Four Democrats and Four Republicans. We drafted comprehensive immigration reform legislation that we were confident had the bipartisan votes to pass the House. The only thing missing was the political will of the Republican Leadership to bring it to the floor.

Beyond addressing humanitarian and security needs, CBO has repeatedly told us that comprehensive immigration reform would mean a larger economy and a smaller budget deficit. It is my hope that my colleagues across the aisle will recognize these facts and enact the immigration reform we so desperately need.

We can't solve the challenges we face as a nation, whether its immigration, health care, the economy, or passing a Congressional budget without acknowledging what got us here and continuing on that path. To return to where we were and abandon all the progress we have made would be devastating not just for American families today, but for generations to come.

Interim Chair BLACK. Thank you, Mr. Yarmuth. In the interest of time, if any other members have opening statements, I ask you to submit them for the record.

I would like now to recognize the director of the CBO, Dr. Keith Hall. Mr. Hall, thank you again for your time today, and the committee has received your written statement, and it will be made part of the formal hearing record. You have 5 minutes to deliver your oral remarks. You may begin when you are ready.

STATEMENT OF KEITH HALL, PH.D, DIRECTOR, CONGRESSIONAL BUDGET OFFICE

Mr. HALL. Thank you. Chairman Black, Ranking Member Yarmuth, and members of the committee, thank you for inviting me to testify about the Congressional Budget Office's most recent analysis of the outlook for the budget and for the economy.

I will discuss a few highlights of our updated budget and economic projections which were released last week. After my brief remarks, I will be happy to take your questions.

The economic forecast that underlies CBO's budget projections indicates that in real terms gross domestic product will expand an average annual pace of 2.1 percent over the next 2 years, if current laws remain generally unchanged, after rising last year at an annual rate of 1.8 percent. We expect that growth to boost employment, virtually eliminate the remaining slack in the economy, and drop the unemployment rate to 4.4 percent by the fourth quarter of 2018.

Further ahead, according to CBO's projections, GDP will expand at an average annual rate of 1.9 percent over the second half of the coming decade. That growth rate represents a significant slowdown from the average over the 1980s, 1990s and early 2000s, mainly because of the slower growth projected for the Nation's supply of labor which largely results from ongoing retirement of baby boomers and the relative stability in the labor force participation rate among working women.

As slack diminishes over the next 2 years, we expect the rate of inflation to rise to the Federal Reserve's goal of 2 percent and to stay there on average. We also anticipate that the Federal Reserve will steadily raise the target for Federal funds and that interest rates over the next few years will be significantly higher than they are now.

CBO's current economic projections differ a bit from those it published in August 2016. The agency now expects GDP in 2016 to be modestly lower than it projected last summer. It also expects lower interest rates in the next 5 years but projects a higher rate of labor force participation throughout the next decade than it projected in August. In fiscal year 2016, for the first time since 2009, the Federal budget deficit increased in relation to GDP.

CBO projects that over the next 10 years, if current laws remain generally unchanged, budget deficits would eventually follow an upward trajectory, the results of three main trends.

First, strong growth in spending for retirement and healthcare programs targeted to older people, especially Social Security and Medicare.

Second, rising interest payments on the government's debt.

And third, modest growth in revenue collections. By the end of the period, the accumulating deficits would drive up debt held by the public from its already high level. Moreover, 3 decades from now, if current laws remain in place, that debt would be nearly twice as high relative to GDP as it is this year and would reach a higher percentage than any previously recorded.

Such high and rising debt would have serious negative consequences for the budget and the Nation including an increased risk of a fiscal crisis.

Our estimate of the deficit for 2017 is lower than our August estimate, primarily because we now expect lower mandatory spending. The current projection of the cumulative deficit for the 2017 to 2026 period, however, is about the same as we published in August.

I am often asked specifically about our projections for Medicaid and Federal subsidies for health insurance purchased through the market places established by the Affordable Care Act. By CBO's estimates, an average of 12 million people under the age of 65 will have health insurance in any given month in 2017 as a result of the expansion of Medicaid under the ACA.

In addition, CBO and the staff of the Joint Committee and Taxation estimate that this year, nine million people per month on average will receive subsidies for nongroup coverage purchased through the marketplaces. An additional 1 million people are projected to be covered by unsubsidized insurance purchased through the marketplaces. We estimate that 27 million people under the age of 65 will be uninsured on average in 2017.

CBO and JCT currently estimate that in 2017, Federal spending for people made eligible for Medicaid covered by the ACA will be $70 billion and that net Federal subsidies for coverage obtained through the marketplaces will be $45 billion. For the entire 10 year period, 2018 to 2027, if current laws remain in place, those two types of costs would total $1.9 trillion. It is important to note CBO's baseline is not intended to be a forecast of what will happen. Rather, it is meant to provide a neutral benchmark that policymakers can use to assess the potential effects of policy decisions.

CBO's budget and economic projections are predicated on the assumption that the laws that are currently governing Federal taxes and spending generally remain in place for the entire projection period. Even if that occurred, and there are no changes in those laws before the end of the period, it would still not be possible to predict budgetary and economic outcomes precisely because many other factors are uncertain.

Our goal is to construct budget and economic projections that fall in the middle of the distribution of possible outcomes given both the fiscal policy embodied in current law and the availability of economic and other data. I would now be happy to answer your questions.

[The prepared statement of Mr. Hall follows:]

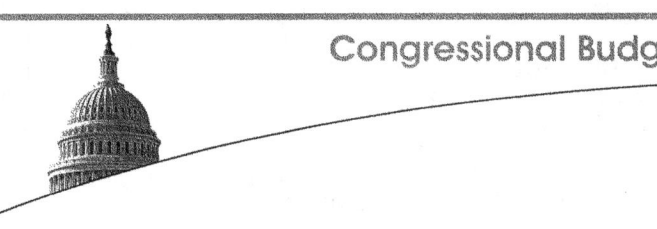

Congressional Budget Office

Testimony

The Budget and Economic Outlook: 2017 to 2027

Keith Hall
Director

Before the
Committee on the Budget
U.S. House of Representatives

February 2, 2017

This document is embargoed until it is delivered at 10:00 a.m. (EST) on Thursday, February 2, 2017. The contents may not be published, transmitted, or otherwise communicated by any print, broadcast, or electronic media before that time.

Chairman Black, Ranking Member Yarmuth, and Members of the Committee, thank you for inviting me to testify about the Congressional Budget Office's most recent analysis of the outlook for the budget and the economy. My statement summarizes CBO's new baseline budget projections and economic forecast, which the agency released last week.[1]

In fiscal year 2016, for the first time since 2009, the federal budget deficit increased in relation to the nation's economic output. CBO projects that over the next decade, if current laws remained generally unchanged, budget deficits would eventually follow an upward trajectory—the result of strong growth in spending for retirement and health care programs targeted to older people and rising interest payments on the government's debt, accompanied by only modest growth in revenue collections. Those accumulating deficits would drive debt held by the public from its already high level up to its highest percentage of gross domestic product (GDP) since shortly after World War II.

CBO's estimate of the deficit for 2017 has decreased since August 2016, when the agency issued its previous estimates, primarily because mandatory spending is expected to be lower than earlier anticipated.[2] However, the current projection for the cumulative deficit for the 2017–2026 period is about the same as that reported in August.

CBO's economic forecast—which underlies its budget projections—indicates that under current law, economic growth over the next two years would remain close to the modest rate observed since the end of the recession in 2009. Nevertheless, economic growth would continue to outpace growth in potential (maximum sustainable) GDP and thus continue to reduce the amount of underused resources, or slack, in the economy. The result would be increases in hiring, employment, and wages, along with upward pressure on inflation and interest rates. In the later part of the 10-year projection period, output growth would be constrained by a relatively slow increase in the nation's supply of labor.

CBO's current economic projections differ from those it published in August because of revisions involving several factors that determine potential output. The agency now expects real (inflation-adjusted) GDP and real potential GDP in 2026 to be modestly lower than projected in August. It also expects interest rates to be lower in the first half of the projection period, but it projects a higher rate of labor force participation throughout the period than it reported in August.

CBO's budget and economic projections are predicated on the assumption that current laws generally remain in place. Budgetary and economic outcomes are difficult to project, however, and thus rather uncertain—even if there are no changes to the laws that govern federal taxes and spending. The agency strives to construct 10-year budget and economic projections that fall in the middle of the distribution of possible outcomes, given both the fiscal policy embodied in current law and the availability of economic and other data.

The Budget Deficit for 2017 Is Projected to Be Similar to Last Year's

CBO's baseline estimate of the 2017 deficit is $559 billion, or 2.9 percent of GDP—less than the $587 billion deficit posted in 2016 (see Table 1). Both totals, however, are affected by shifts in the timing of some payments. Outlays in 2016—and thus the deficit—were boosted by $41 billion because certain payments that were to be made on October 1, 2016 (the first day of fiscal year 2017), were instead made in fiscal year 2016 because October 1 fell on a weekend.[3]

For 2017, the net effect of those timing shifts and similar shifts in spending from fiscal year 2018 into fiscal year 2017 is to increase outlays by $4 billion. If not for those shifts, the deficit in 2016 would have been $546 billion (3.0 percent of GDP), and the deficit projected for 2017 would be $555 billion (2.9 percent of GDP).

If there are no further legislative changes, both revenues and outlays (adjusted to eliminate the timing shifts) are

1. Congressional Budget Office, *The Budget and Economic Outlook: 2017 to 2027* (January 2017), www.cbo.gov/publication/52370.

2. See Congressional Budget Office, *An Update to the Budget and Economic Outlook: 2016 to 2026* (August 2016), www.cbo.gov/publication/51908.

3. October 1 will fall on a weekend again in 2017, 2022, and 2023. In such cases, certain payments due on October 1 are made at the end of September and thus are recorded in the previous fiscal year. Those shifts noticeably boosted projected spending and deficits in fiscal year 2016 and, in CBO's projections, increase them in 2022; the timing shifts reduce federal spending and deficits in fiscal years 2018 and 2024.

Table 1.

CBO's Baseline Budget Projections

	Actual, 2016	2017	2018	2019	2020	2021	2022	2023	2024	2025	2026	2027	Total 2018-2022	Total 2018-2027
							In Billions of Dollars							
Revenues	3,267	3,404	3,604	3,733	3,878	4,019	4,176	4,346	4,527	4,724	4,931	5,140	19,410	43,078
Outlays	3,854	3,963	4,091	4,334	4,562	4,816	5,135	5,346	5,554	5,890	6,228	6,548	22,938	52,504
Deficit	-587	-559	-487	-601	-684	-797	-959	-1,000	-1,027	-1,165	-1,297	-1,408	-3,528	-9,426
Debt Held by the Public at the End of the Year	14,168	14,838	15,416	16,092	16,845	17,704	18,721	19,776	20,858	22,078	23,430	24,893	n.a.	n.a.
							As a Percentage of Gross Domestic Product							
Revenues	17.8	17.8	18.1	18.1	18.1	18.1	18.1	18.1	18.2	18.2	18.3	18.4	18.1	18.2
Outlays	20.9	20.7	20.5	21.0	21.3	21.7	22.3	22.3	22.3	22.8	23.1	23.4	21.4	22.2
Deficit	-3.2	-2.9	-2.4	-2.9	-3.2	-3.6	-4.2	-4.2	-4.1	-4.5	-4.8	-5.0	-3.3	-4.0
Debt Held by the Public at the End of the Year	77.0	77.5	77.4	77.9	78.8	79.9	81.3	82.6	83.8	85.3	87.0	88.9	n.a.	n.a.

Source: Congressional Budget Office.

n.a. = not applicable.

projected to rise by about 4 percent this year. Higher receipts from individual income taxes would be responsible for much of the projected revenue increase, and net interest payments would be the fastest-growing component of the increase in spending.

Outlays (if not for the timing shifts) and revenues would both rise at about the same rate as GDP, CBO estimates, so they would be roughly the same relative to the size of the economy in 2016 and 2017: 20.7 percent for outlays and 17.8 percent for revenues. Debt held by the public is projected to rise slightly relative to GDP.

Growing Deficits Through 2027 Are Projected to Drive Up Federal Debt

In CBO's baseline projections, budget deficits remain below 3.0 percent of GDP through 2019. But subsequently, continued growth in spending—particularly for Social Security, Medicare, and net interest—would outstrip growth in revenues, resulting in larger deficits and increasing debt. By 2027, the deficit would reach 5.0 percent of GDP—$1.4 trillion.

Revenues

If current laws generally remained unchanged, revenues would rise from 17.8 percent of GDP in 2017 to 18.4 percent by 2027. They have averaged 17.4 percent of GDP over the past 50 years.

Only revenues from individual income taxes would grow faster than the economy over the course of the decade. CBO's baseline includes the following projections:

- Receipts from individual income taxes increase by a total of 1.1 percentage points of GDP over the 10-year period as a result of several factors, including real bracket creep (the process by which, as income rises faster than prices, an ever-larger proportion of income becomes subject to higher tax rates), rising distributions from tax-deferred retirement accounts, and an increase in the share of wages and salaries earned by higher-income taxpayers.

- Remittances from the Federal Reserve, which have been unusually high since 2010, drop by 0.2 percentage points of GDP to return to more typical amounts.

- Payroll tax receipts decline by 0.1 percentage point of GDP, primarily because of the expected increase in the share of wages going to higher-income taxpayers.

- Corporate income tax receipts as a share of GDP also fall by 0.1 percentage point between 2017 and 2027.

Figure 1.

Federal Debt Held by the Public

Percentage of Gross Domestic Product

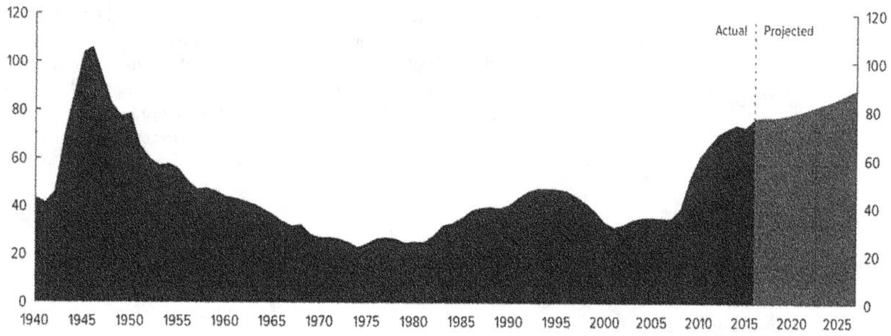

Source: Congressional Budget Office.

Outlays

In CBO's projections, outlays remain near 21 percent of GDP for the next few years, which is higher than their average of 20.3 percent over the past 50 years. Later in the coming decade, the growth in outlays would exceed growth in the economy, and, by 2027, outlays would rise to 23.4 percent of GDP. That increase reflects significant growth in mandatory spending and interest payments, which is offset somewhat by a decline in discretionary spending as a share of GDP. More specifically, CBO's baseline includes the following projections:

- Outlays for mandatory programs increase as a share of GDP by 2.4 percentage points from 2017 to 2027—mainly because of the aging of the population and rising per capita health care costs. Social Security and Medicare account for nearly all of that increase.
- Because of rising interest rates and, to a lesser extent, growing federal debt held by the public, the government's interest payments on that debt rise sharply over the next 10 years—nearly tripling in nominal terms and almost doubling relative to GDP.
- Discretionary spending drops from 6.3 percent of GDP in 2017 to 5.3 percent in 2027—a smaller percentage relative to the size of the economy than in any year since 1962 (the first year for which comparable data are available).

Debt Held by the Public

As deficits accumulate in CBO's baseline, debt held by the public rises from 77 percent of GDP ($15 trillion) at the end of 2017 to 89 percent of GDP ($25 trillion) by 2027. At that level, debt held by the public would be the largest since 1947 and more than twice the average over the past five decades in relation to GDP (see Figure 1).

Beyond the 10-year period, if current laws remained in place, the pressures that contributed to rising deficits during the baseline period would accelerate and push debt up even more sharply. Three decades from now, for instance, debt held by the public is projected to be nearly twice as high, relative to GDP, as it is this year—and a higher percentage than any previously recorded.

Such high and rising debt would have serious negative consequences for the budget and the nation:

- Federal spending on interest payments would increase substantially as a result of increases in interest rates, such as those projected to occur over the next few years.
- Because federal borrowing reduces total saving in the economy over time, the nation's capital stock would ultimately be smaller, and productivity and total wages would be lower.

- Lawmakers would have less flexibility to use tax and spending policies to respond to unexpected challenges.

- The likelihood of a fiscal crisis in the United States would increase. There would be a greater risk that investors would become unwilling to finance the government's borrowing unless they were compensated with very high interest rates; if that happened, interest rates on federal debt would rise suddenly and sharply.

The Projected Deficit for 2017 Is Smaller Than CBO's August 2016 Estimate, but the Cumulative Deficit Is Largely Unchanged

The deficit that CBO now projects for 2017 is $35 billion less than the amount the agency estimated in August. Revenues and outlays alike are expected to be lower: revenues by $17 billion, mostly as a result of lower receipts from individual income taxes, and outlays by $52 billion, mostly because of reductions in mandatory spending.

For the 2017–2026 period, CBO now projects a cumulative deficit that is just $6 billion (or less than 0.1 percent) larger than it projected in August, and the total remains at $8.6 trillion for that period. By 2026, debt held by the public is projected to total $23 trillion, about the same as in the August projections.

CBO Expects Moderate Economic Growth to Continue

According to CBO's current baseline projections, continued economic expansion over the next two years will virtually eliminate slack in the economy, thus putting upward pressure on inflation and interest rates. After that, the economy is expected to grow a bit more slowly. The projections for later years do not reflect predictions about business-cycle fluctuations or possible changes in fiscal policy; rather, they are based primarily on projected trends of underlying factors, such as productivity, growth in the labor force and in the number of hours worked, inflation, and interest rates.

Economic Growth

CBO estimates that, in real terms, GDP will expand at an average annual pace of 2.1 percent from the fourth quarter of 2016 to the fourth quarter of 2018, after having risen at an annual rate of 1.8 percent last year (see Figure 2). Most of the growth in output during the coming years will be driven by consumer spending, business investment, and residential construction, CBO anticipates.

According to CBO's projections, actual and potential GDP alike will expand at an average annual rate of 1.9 percent during the second half of the 10-year period. CBO estimates that the growth of potential output over that period will be faster than it has been since the 2007–2009 recession, mainly because the productivity of the labor force is projected to rise, returning closer to its average of the preceding two decades. However, that rate of output growth represents a significant slowdown from the average over the 1980s, 1990s, and early 2000s, mainly because of the slower growth projected for the nation's supply of labor, which is largely attributable to the ongoing retirement of baby boomers and the relatively stable labor force participation rate among working-age women. (The labor force participation rate is the percentage of people in the civilian noninstitutionalized population who are at least 16 years old and are either working or seeking work.)

The Labor Market

The shortfall between actual and potential employment, CBO's primary measure of slack in the labor market, was about 1.6 million people at the end of 2016.[4] That shortfall is projected to disappear in 2018 as the result of two developments. First, the strengthening economy is expected to slow the downward trend in the rate of labor force participation as the increase in employers' demand for labor continues to draw workers back into the labor force. Second, increases in hiring will lower the unemployment rate, which is projected to reach 4.4 percent by the end of 2018. As slack in the labor market dissipates over the next two years, hourly wages are expected to rise.

Over the next five years, the monthly increase in nonfarm payroll employment, which is estimated to average 160,000 jobs in the first half of 2017, is projected to settle down to an average of 64,000 jobs. That slower pace of job growth primarily reflects relatively slow growth in the labor force, which is affected by the ongoing retirement of the baby boomers. In CBO's projections, the

4. Potential employment is the number of people employed when unemployment is at its natural rate—the rate that arises from all sources except fluctuations in aggregate demand—and when labor force participation is at its potential rate. (Aggregate demand is the overall demand for goods and services in the economy.)

Figure 2.

Actual Values and CBO's Projections of Key Economic Indicators

CBO projects that economic activity will expand at a pace this year and next that will lower the unemployment rate and place upward pressure on inflation and interest rates.

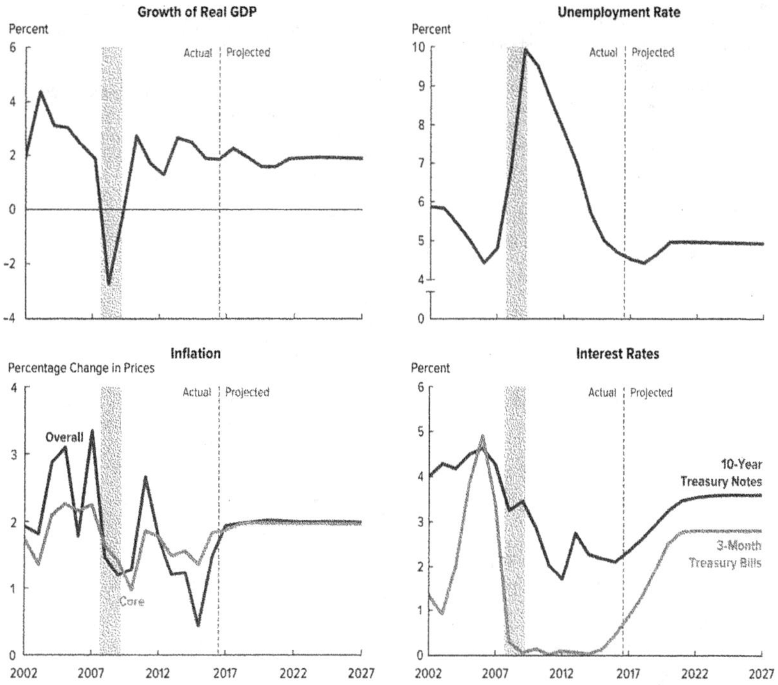

Source: Congressional Budget Office, using data from the Bureau of Economic Analysis, the Bureau of Labor Statistics, and the Federal Reserve.

Real GDP is the output of the economy adjusted to remove the effects of inflation. The unemployment rate is a measure of the number of jobless people who are available for work and are actively seeking jobs, expressed as a percentage of the labor force. The overall inflation rate is based on the price index for personal consumption expenditures; the core rate excludes prices for food and energy.

For real GDP growth and inflation, percentage changes are measured from the fourth quarter of one calendar year to the fourth quarter of the next. For the unemployment and interest rates, data are fourth-quarter values.

GDP = gross domestic product.

unemployment rate averages 4.9 percent over the later part of the projection period.

Inflation

CBO expects prices to rise at a modest pace over the next few years. The agency anticipates that the diminishing slack in the economy and higher oil prices will put upward pressure on prices for goods and services. That pressure will be somewhat alleviated by the effects of a strong dollar in relation to other currencies, which will reduce the cost of imported goods. In CBO's projections, the rate of inflation, as measured by the price index for personal consumption expenditures, rises to 1.9 percent in 2017 and to 2.0 percent in 2018. It remains, on average, at the Federal Reserve's longer-run goal of 2 percent throughout the rest of the coming decade.

Interest Rates

As the slack in the economy continues to diminish, the Federal Reserve will continue to reduce its support of economic growth, in CBO's view. Thus, the federal funds rate—the interest rate that financial institutions charge one another for overnight loans of their monetary reserves—is expected to rise gradually over the next few years, reaching 1.1 percent in the fourth quarter of 2017, 1.6 percent in the fourth quarter of 2018, and 3.1 percent in the later part of the projection period. Interest rates on short-term Treasury securities are expected to follow a similar pattern.

A projected rise in longer-term rates reflects the anticipated increase in short-term rates and an expected increase in the term premium from historically low levels. (The term premium is paid to bondholders as compensation for the extra risk associated with longer-term securities.) In CBO's estimation, the term premium has remained low because of heightened concern about global economic growth and increased demand for longer-term Treasury securities as a hedge against possible economic adversity. CBO projects that the interest rate on 10-year Treasury notes will rise from 2.1 percent in the fourth quarter of 2016 to 3.6 percent in the later part of the projection period.

Although CBO projects that interest rates will rise above those currently in effect, they are projected to remain low by historical standards, for several reasons: slower growth in the labor force, slightly slower growth in productivity, and only partial dissipation of the factors that have increased the demand for Treasury securities and held down the term premium.

Real GDP Is Projected to Be Modestly Lower Than CBO Estimated in August

CBO's current economic projections differ somewhat from those the agency made in August 2016. Most significantly, potential and actual real GDP are expected to grow more slowly. As a result, those measures are 0.8 percent lower than CBO previously projected for 2026 (the last year in the previous projection period). CBO's projection of economic output is lower because of improvements in the agency's analytical methods and because of data that became available between early July and early December 2016. Nominal GDP is expected to be a little lower, on average, over the decade.

Other changes are relatively small. CBO now estimates that over the next decade, more people will be working than it estimated in August. That change results from an upward revision to the projected labor force participation rate, which is partially offset by a downward revision in the projected size of the population. Also, interest rates are expected to be lower in the first half of the decade than they were in the August projections. The slower rise in interest rates that CBO now projects stems partly from an anticipated slowing in the pace of rate increases by the Federal Reserve.

This testimony reiterates the summary of *The Budget and Economic Outlook: 2017 to 2027*, which is one in a series of reports on the state of the budget and the economy that CBO issues each year. The report satisfies the requirement of section 202(e) of the Congressional Budget Act of 1974 for CBO to submit to the Committees on the Budget periodic reports about fiscal policy and to provide baseline projections of the federal budget. In accordance with CBO's mandate to provide objective, impartial analysis, neither that report nor this testimony makes any recommendations. Both publications are available on CBO's website, at www.cbo.gov/publication/52370 and www.cbo.gov/publication/52390, respectively.

Keith Hall
Director

Interim Chair BLACK. Thank you, Mr. Hall. Now, we will begin the question and answer session. If I could ask the staff to bring up Figure 5 from my first question. Mr. Hall, CBO's economic forecast has been trending sharply downward in the recent years, and roughly 5 years ago, CBO was expecting real GDP growth to average around three percent over the 10 year budget horizon. Close to that long-term average growth rate that we have seen here in the U.S., that figure has been dropping consistently, and in this latest forecast, it is down to just 1.9 percent.

So, it seems that CBO is expecting that the U.S. economy will experience a protracted economic malaise for at least the next decade under current policies. So, two questions I have for you. First of all, what are the reasons for CBO keep ratcheting down its projections for the GDP growth, and secondly, how will this much lower expected growth path affect our Federal budget?

Mr. HALL. They look forward over the next 10 years. We do expect the slack in the economy to be virtually eliminated over the next 2 years, so we will be on what we think is the potential growth of GDP, and what is constraining the potential growth of GDP as we forecast it something like 1.8, 1.9 percent, is a combination of a more slowly growing labor force. A lot of that is an aging population as baby boomers retire, not all of it, however, and slower productivity growth.

Since the end of the recession, productivity growth has only been 0.8 percent, so it is less than 1 percent productivity growth. We expect that will go up by the end of the period as something like 1.3 percent, but that is still lower than it has been in the past. So, in fact, if you sort of take that labor force of growing 0.5 percent, productivity growing 1.3 percent, add those together, that 1.8 percent, 1.9 percent is about our economic forecast. And so, the challenges are slower growing labor force and slower growing productivity, and again we have this issue with baby boomers in particular that we have seen coming for a long time. It is just starting to get closer and closer now.

Interim Chair BLACK. How do you expect what you are projecting up here to affect the Federal budget?

Mr. HALL. Well, this is going to have an impact. This is going make, it is going to contribute probably to the growth in the deficit going forward. Something like productivity, for example, which is part of what is at the heart here, has a pretty significant impact on our budget forecast, so if we get some increase, for example in productivity, we will have a smaller growing deficit, but the problem is so big that even that is not really going to solve the problem.

Interim Chair BLACK. So, to the other end of that, coupled with this sluggish economy is the relentless rise in our government spending and deficits. And your figures show that the tax revenues are already above the 50 year averages of percentage of DDP and are projected to keep growing, and yet our spending keeps growing faster. If we tried to balance the budget just by raising taxes, how big would the tax increase be required in order to be able to catch up?

Mr. HALL. Well, just to give you some idea. We have actually got a great little Figure 17, and it gives you some idea of the size of the deficit relative to the size of things like revenues and discretionary spending and etc. We see the deficit in 10 years it is going to be about $1.4 trillion. That is about 5 percent of GDP, and total revenues are going to be about 18 percent of GDP in 10 years. So, it is a major chunk of revenues right now. So, it would be a pretty significant increase in revenues to get there.

Interim Chair BLACK. Any idea of what percent we would have to increase taxes in order to be able to get there?

Mr. HALL. We have not done a scenario like that.

Interim Chair BLACK. But significant is what you are saying.

Mr. HALL. It would be significant, and it would probably also significantly change our economic forecast as well, so it makes it particularly complicated.

Interim Chair BLACK. So, even for those who would favor some combination of spending restraint and tax increases, is it fair to say that getting control of spending is really indispensable in this equation to overcome those chronic deficits and debt?

Mr. HALL. Well, that seems to be the picture. The growing deficit and the growing debt is so large it is hard to imagine just picking on either revenues or outlays and not looking at both things, and the broader you look, the smaller the change you need. So, if you restrict yourself to just smaller buckets, for example, just discretionary spending, you really got to reduce discretionary spending. So, that is clearly one of the features here that we see that this is a really big hole to fill.

Interim Chair BLACK. So, on the other side of that. If we could achieve a more robust degree of economic growth, say something closer to that historic average of just a little over 3 percent, how much would that help us in shrinking those deficits?

Mr. HALL. I will give you a little bit of an idea. We do not have GDP in here, but we have a little scenario with productivity growth. For every one-tenth of a percentage point in productivity growth, we see the deficit in 10 years shrinking by about $50 billion. So, something like an increase in productivity of a half a percentage point would be pretty significant, and that is going to reduce the deficit by about a $250 million and that is out of a $1.4 trillion deficit. So, that makes a difference, but it is, even a half a percentage point is not enough to balance the budget essentially in 10 years.

Interim Chair BLACK. Let me go to another topic. Let's go to Figure 2, please. One of the most troubling aspects of our CBO's outlook is the stubbornly low rate of labor workforce participation. That rate now stands at 62.7 percent close to a 40-year low, and CBO expects this to continue declining over this next decade which is just really disappointing. Obviously, the ongoing retirement of baby boomers generation plays a key role, but CBO also states that government policies are exacerbating the trend. Is it correct that the labor force is a key component of economic growth, and how large does that role play, and second to that is, what are some of the policies that do affect this, and how do they crease incentives for work?

Mr. HALL. Sure. I would say if you look at the long run growth of the economy, long run health of the economy, you can look at two different things. You can look at labor force growth, and you can look at productivity growth. If you compare our growth that we see over the next 10 years to what we had in the 1990s when we had 3.3 percent GDP, the slowdown of labor force growth is about half that difference.

So, it is pretty significant, and you are right, although baby boomers retiring is a source of that decline in labor force participation, we also have lower labor force participation by every cohort in the United States. And, that is certainly one of the targets I think for having sort of a supply side impact that raises potential GDP is doing things to increase the labor force participation by working age people.

Interim Chair BLACK. What kind of policies can we initiate to change this tragectory?

Mr. HALL. Well, certainly we have identified, we often do, we point out what amounts to implicit taxes on work. There are a number of things that are implicit taxes on work where we reduce benefits when income goes up. The ACA itself probably reduces labor force participation. That is a drag as well. There are a number of things like that. I do not want to get too specific about it, but just the sort of things that will get people back into the workforce are things that will help that labor force participation and help this potential GDP growth problem that we have.

Interim Chair BLACK. I do thank you for all of your comments on this, and I will go back to my opening remarks as I conclude my time, that it really bothers me so much that we have people who are out of the workforce because I know from my career and my children and so on, that work is good for the soul. And I often tell people that after you ask someone, you say hello, this is my name, what is the second question you ask them? What do you do? And if you are productive and you are feeling good about your work and what you are contributing to society, that overall helps the entire society.

And so, this is for me even more about how we have our society grow as a society that is whole and healthy as much as it is and what it will do to help keep the economy going. All of this together is what makes our country great. Thank you, and I now yield to the ranking member, Mr. Yarmuth.

Mr. YARMUTH. Thank you, Chairman Black. I am going to defer my questions to later in the hearing.

Interim Chair BLACK. So, who came into the room? Oh, it is coming. Okay. Would you like to yield to one of your members?

Mr. YARMUTH. Sure. I would like to.

Chairman BLACK. You know, that was here first.

Mr. YARMUTH. All right, Mr. Jeffries from New York was here first, so I will yield to him.

Interim Chair BLACK. Mr. Jeffries, you are recognized for 5 minutes.

Mr. JEFFRIES. Thank you, chair, and thank the distinguished ranking member for yielding. A statement was made earlier that we can chose to get the economy working again. I want to pursue that for a moment, because I think that the economy has been working ever since the turnaround that we engineered by the previous President 8 years ago. Is not it in fact the case that when Barack Obama came into office this country was in a mess and in the danger of total collapse?

Mr. HALL. Well, that is right. We were undergoing significant job loss and decline in GDP growth.

Mr. JEFFRIES. Stock market was a mess. Correct?

Mr. HALL. Yes.

Mr. JEFFRIES. Automobile industry a mess. Correct?

Mr. HALL. Yes.

Mr. JEFFRIES. Bank industry a mess. Correct?

Mr. HALL. Yes.

Mr. JEFFRIES. 401k is a mess. Correct?

Mr. HALL. Yes.

Mr. JEFFRIES. Housing market a mess. Correct?

Mr. HALL. Yes.

Mr. JEFFRIES. And since 2010, this country has gained more than 15 million private sector jobs. Is that right?

Mr. HALL. I think that is right.

Mr. JEFFRIES. Eight years ago, the stock market was around 6,000. Is that right?

Mr. HALL. That sounds right.

Mr. JEFFRIES. And now it is over 19,000. Is that correct?

Mr. HALL. Yes.

Mr. JEFFRIES. Eight years ago, the unemployment rate was at over 10 percent. Is that right?

Mr. HALL. Yes.

Mr. JEFFRIES. And now it is under 5 percent. Is that correct?

Mr. HALL. Yes.

Mr. JEFFRIES. The deficit has been reduced by more than a trillion dollars over the last 8 years, correct?

Mr. HALL. That sounds right.

Mr. JEFFRIES. Okay. So, the statement about getting the economy working again I think perhaps is inaccurate as a snapshot of what actually has occurred over the last 8 years, and so it seems that what we need to do is build upon the tremendous progress that has been made under the leadership of Barack Obama and keep this country moving forward. I would also note on this question of whether we should cooperate with the new President, that Barack Obama was able to lead an economic turnaround without an ounce of cooperation from the other side who decided to pursue an agenda of obstruction today, obstruction tomorrow, obstruction forever over the last 8 years and so hopefully we can find ourselves in a situation where we move forward in a cooperative fashion in a way that benefits all of America. In terms of our present situation, the CBO expects that economic growth will be sluggish over the next decade. Is that right?

Mr. HALL. That is correct.

Mr. JEFFRIES. And in part that is because of a decline in labor force participation. Correct?

Mr. HALL. That is correct.

Mr. JEFFRIES. Now, would the retirement that will continue of baby boomers out of the labor workforce exacerbate this problem in a way that will continue to provide modest, if not sluggish, economic growth moving forward over the next 10 years?

Mr. HALL. That is right. It is almost certainly going to happen and certainly going to be a difficulty in achieving higher economic growth.

Mr. JEFFRIES. And this is a problem that Japan for instance which had a booming economy in the 1980s is experiencing today. Is that true?

Mr. HALL. That is true.

Mr. JEFFRIES. And one of the reasons why Japan in experiencing that problem is because they got very harsh immigration policies, and they do not have the natural growth from their own population that would lead to robust participation in the labor force. Is that right?

Mr. HALL. Yes.

Mr. JEFFRIES. So, there was a comprehensive immigration reform bill that I think was passed by the Senate in 2013. Mr. Yarmuth mentioned it worked hard to get it enacted into law here in the House, but due to the politics of the situation, it did not go anywhere. I believe the CBO studied that particular piece of legislation and concluded that over about a 20 year period it will reduce the deficit I think by $700 billion. Is that right?

Mr. HALL. That sounds right.

Mr. JEFFRIES. So, it would have a positive impact, comprehensive immigration reform, on our economic situation. Correct?

Mr. HALL. That is right. It is primarily through increased growth in the labor force. So, that is one of the primary constraint going forward is the growth in the labor force.

Mr. JEFFRIES. And one of the ways that we can deal with the labor force moving forward is to make sure that our immigration policies continue to welcome individuals who come to America, work hard, will contribute to the labor force since we are not naturally able to produce the numbers that would result in increased economic productivity. Is that a fair statement?

Mr. HALL. It probably is, although keep in mind the effects of any particular labor immigration policy can be complicated, so we would have to sort of see exactly what is being proposed, but there is one constant in that it does affect the labor supply and that labor supply does help GDP growth.

Mr. JEFFRIES. Okay. Thank you. I yield back.

Interim Chair BLACK. The gentleman from Oklahoma is recognized. Mr. Cole.

Mr. COLE. Thank you, Madam Chairman, and thank you, Mr. Director, for your testimony. It is always good to have you here. I want to focus in on this trendline in terms of the deficit just a little bit, and we as you know think of the Federal budget in two different pots, discretionary and mandatory spending, mandatory being primarily Social Security, Medicare, Medicaid, the classic entitlement programs." What has been the trendline on discretionary spending over the last few years?

Mr. HALL. Well, discretionary spending is looking like it is going to decline as a share of GDP. It has been declining, so in fact while we look forward to the next 10 years and see spending increase really significantly, discretionary spending is not increasing significantly, and that in fact is declining as a share of GDP.

Mr. COLE. As a share of GDP and since 2009 it has actually declined very substantially in real terms just as an amount. I mean we were actually spending considerably less on the discretionary portions of the budget and that is everything from defense to NASA to National Institutes of Health than we were in 2009 and 2010. Is that correct?

Mr. HALL. That is correct, yes.

Mr. COLE. Give us the trendline if you would on mandatory spending, again the classic entitlement programs. What has that trend been in the last 5 or 6 years? Where do you see it going over the next decade?

Mr. HALL. Well, mandatory spending continues to grow faster than GDP, quite a bit faster. Ever, you know, the revenues are growing as a share of GDP, but spending especially mandatory spending is growing a lot fast. So, it is sort of a race that mandatory spending is winning in adding to the deficit going forward.

Mr. COLE. And are there any significant proposals out there on either side of the aisle to change the direction of that, slow it down, manage it a little bit better?

Mr. HALL. Nothing comes to mind. You know, one of the things I like to point out, we just produced something called options for reducing the deficit. Sort of a nice thick volume with over a hundred options, and we give you some options on things like mandatory spending and other things that you can look at for reducing the deficit going forward. It gives you some idea of how much of an impact those different options would have.

Mr. COLE. When was the last time we had significant reform in, let's say Social Security?

Mr. HALL. I think it has been a while. I am not an expert in Social Security. There have been some adjustments in benefits in delaying eligibility and some things like that, but they still have not affected the long-run problem that we have seen coming for decades. It is still coming.

Mr. COLE. I think the last time we really made much progress in this area was actually very bipartisan, and it was with President Reagan, and the House was Democratic in the period. Tip O'Neill, Howard Baker in the Senate. In other words, they came together, set up a commission and extended the life of Social Security fairly dramatic in the middle 1980s. We have not really gone back and done too much since then. Is that correct as you recall?

Mr. HALL. That is correct.

Mr. COLE. I say this in a very self-serving way because my friend, Mr. Delaney, on the other side, and I have a bill that would set up another commission that would be, by nature, bipartisan. It would be 7 and 6. We actually have introduced it in a couple of Congresses. Seven members chosen effectively by the President and the majority party, six by the minority, but you would have to have nine votes to actually report something to Congress. Congress would then have about 60 days to vote it up or down, and I would invite my colleagues on both sides of the aisle just to look at that legislation because I think if you read the numbers, which you so accurately and persuasively put out here, sooner or later we have to address mandatory spending.

Neither side in the last campaign did that in any meaningful way. Neither side, frankly, in the House and the Senate has actually advanced legislation. We actually always write a budget that addresses this, and I hope we do that again, Madam Chairman. I hope we do not ignore the elephant in the room, so to speak, and

I am sure we will not under your leadership and my good friend and ranking member I know has these same concerns. But I know I am not using the question, but I do want to finish and then I will yield back. I just would invite my colleagues.

We can score points against one another all day. We both have great arguments and great talking points. This is a problem we could solve. It is a math problem. It is not as tough as Medicare and Medicaid. We literally could sit down and negotiate this through just as President Reagan and Speaker O'Neill did and Howard Baker, and I would invite us to begin that process because I do not like the way your numbers look at the end of the decade. With that, I yield back. I thank you very much. I thank you for your indulgence, Madam Chairman.

Interim Chair BLACK. Thank the gentleman from Oklahoma. The gentleman from Massachusetts, Mr. Moulton is recognized for 5 minutes.

Mr. MOULTON. Thank you, Madam Chair. I would just like to begin by echoing the comments from Representative Cole because I think you are right. Sometimes people ask me about what it is like to serve on the Budget Committee and I say it is often a great place for people who do not do math. If we started doing math, we could solve a lot of problems. So, thank you, Mr. Cole.

Director Hall, as I am sure you know, immigration has become a major topic of discussion following President Trump's executive order last week. Now, there is a lot of evidence that the order is unconstitutional and it is certainly hurting our national security overseas. Secretary Mattis and others have made that clear, but it is also having a detrimental impact on our economy here at home. The concern, of course, is that with this executive order, the Trump administration is scaring away some of the very people we need to continue growing the economy as our labor force shrinks.

Now, many of America's major corporations and businesses were founded by immigrants. For example, Steve Jobs. His father came from Syria. Apparently, more than half of the current crop of U.S. based startups valued at a billion dollar or more. So, more than half of the current startups with a valuation of billion dollars or more. Collectively, these 44 companies are valued at 168 billion.

They were started by immigrants.

So, $168 billion of valuation creating 33,440 jobs in the U.S. market and immigrants in these companies make up more than 70 percent of key management or product development positions. So, we have heard in the past weeks CEOs from Facebook, Starbucks, Goldman Sachs and other leaders in the business community who have already stated that this ban will hurt their ability to attract and retain talent, and that it may spur people or companies to discount the U.S. as a place to pursue business and investment opportunities. Colleges and universities have also raised alarms, including those in my district, about the impact that this will have on students and faculty who hail from the seven countries targeted by the order.

In 2016, international students in U.S. colleges surpassed 1 million for the first time, contributing more than $32 billion a year to our economy. Thirty-two billion dollars a year, Madam Chair, would certainly help with our budget deficit. That is the kind of consumer spending that we need because it creates jobs.

So, I want to speak briefly about the impact on our healthcare system because more than a quarter of the physician workforce in the U.S. comes from other countries with more than 8,400 doctors working in the U.S. from two countries listed in the executive orders, Syria and Iran alone. Now, we want those talented doctors to be here saving American lives and helping our healthcare system at a time of physician shortage. America does not currently produce enough physicians to keep up with demands. We have a current deficit of over 8,200 primary care doctors. So, that deficit would literally double if the doctors from Iran and Syria were not here.

And so, Director Hall, I know you cannot speak directly to the effects of this executive order as it was just released, but based on the 2013 CBO report on immigration reform and other work that CBO has done on this issue, can you talk in general terms about the impact that such restrictive immigration policies might have on the growth of our economy?

Mr. HALL. Well, you raise an interesting aspect of immigration. And one of the reasons why we really kind of need to see specific proposals is because the type of proposal has different kinds of effects. The evidence is, for example, that increased immigration of unskilled workers probably has an effect in lowering wages for lower skilled workers in the United States. However, when you go to the skilled workers, they in fact increase productivity because as you say there are a lot of entrepreneurs, etc. who are immigrants and skilled immigrants, so that has sort of a different sort of side effect.

Mr. MOULTON. Right, and if you look at the countries in the order like Iran and Syria, are they mostly skilled or unskilled workers who are coming to the U.S.

Mr. HALL. I do not know offhand.

Mr. MOULTON. It is mostly skilled workers. Disproportionately, entrepreneurs and business people. Thank you. Please continue.

Mr. HALL. Okay. Sure. So, you know, if you look at immigration proposals it makes a difference if you are just going to broadly increase immigration. If you are going to increase immigration that is focused more on skilled workers that has sort of a different effect than if it is unskilled workers. The fundamental that our increased labor supply is there, it is sort of the other effects that depend upon exactly who is immigrating, and then of course the size of these would be pretty significant. It is not clear that the executive order that, at least from what I have seen, that that is large enough to make us change our forecast.

Mr. MOULTON. Thank you, sir.

Interim Chair BLACK. The gentleman's time has expired. The gentleman from California, Mr. McClintock is recognized for 5 minutes.

Mr. MCCLINTOCK. Thank you, Madam Chairman. There seems to be two dominant themes coming from my friends across the aisle. One is that the Obama economy has been wonderful and second, we need more foreign immigration to compete for American jobs.

As to the first, I give them the same advice I tried to offer them at our last meeting on Obamacare. Every American has an up close and personal experience with the economy. They know what is going on in their own lives, and any politician who tries to convince them otherwise looks downright foolish. Some people are doing very well in the Obama economy, most people are not. If most people were doing well in this economy, the Democrats would not have lost 67 U.S. House seats, 13 U.S. Senate seats, 11 U.S. governors and more than 900 State legislative seats, not to mention the presidency over the past four election cycles. Just a word of unsolicited advice. Second, with respect to foreign immigration, our foreign immigration over the last decade has been unprecedented.

If my friends were correct, this should be the golden age of the American economy. The impact has been very clear. Badly depressed wages for working families and the lowest labor participation rate since Jimmy Carter. But that is not what I want to talk about. What I want to talk about is what Admiral Mike Mullen warned us was in his professional military judgment, the greatest single threat to our national security, and that was our Nation's debt. And that warning was issued about 5 years and about $4 trillion of debt ago. You report that the debt held by the public this year is 77 percent, but actually our total debt is well over 100 percent of our gross domestic product. Is it not?

Mr. HALL. Well, we look at debt held by the public because that is the important debt for the economy.

Mr. MCCLINTOCK. I know you do, but I think that is highly deceptive. The difference is mainly because Social Security as it runs chronic deficits, we pay back what we borrowed by going to the public for further borrowing. So, what we have got in that overall debt number is in effect converting intragovernmental debt into debt held by the public. Is not that what is going on?

Mr. HALL. Well, that is right. To get to your number.

Mr. MCCLINTOCK. So, we are so deceptively understating the problem since unless we change the law, that gross debt which is now over 100 percent of GDP is destined to become debt held by the public over the next few years. Is not that correct?

Mr. HALL. Well, let me put it this way. The debt held by the public is going to grow really significantly.

Mr. MCCLINTOCK. It is already baked into our total debt which is simply converting the debt we owe to Social Security by borrowing from the public. That is already in those numbers as long as Social Security continues its chronic deficit, that is going to continue, and that is going to require a change in laws. Is it not?

Mr. HALL. That would, yes.

Mr. MCCLINTOCK. So, we are already approaching uncharted territory for this Nation, and the question I have is that on our current trajectory, are we courting a sovereign debt crisis?

Mr. HALL. We are. One of the difficulties is, I cannot tell you exactly.

Mr. MCCLINTOCK. What does that crisis look like?

Mr. HALL. Well, as the debt continues to grow, interest rates when they go back up to normal ranges, we are going to have a major share of our budget just paying off interest. So, that is going to be a real drain.

Mr. MCCLINTOCK. So, would that affect our ability to provide basic services?

Mr. HALL. It will. It is going to reduce flexibility.

Mr. MCCLINTOCK. Would it imperil our ability to respond to a military challenge on the magnitude that we faced after Pearl Harbor?

Mr. HALL. Yeah, absolutely. Our ability to spend money is going to be really limited.

Mr. MCCLINTOCK. How would it affect our overall economy?

Mr. HALL. Well, part of what is going to happen is this is a drag. This is an increase of interest rates. A lot of Federal borrowing crowds out private borrowing, so we actually have lower economic growth.

Mr. MCCLINTOCK. In other words, when the Federal Government borrows a dollar, it borrows it from that same capital market that would otherwise be available to loan to consumers to make consumer purchasers, to businesses to expand jobs. Is that correct?

Mr. HALL. That is correct.

Mr. MCCLINTOCK. Home buyers to buy new homes?

Mr. HALL. That is correct.

Mr. MCCLINTOCK. Taxes are often suggested as an antidote to debt, but are not debt and taxes the same thing? I mean, after we have spent a dollar, have not we already decided to tax it. The only question is whether we tax it now through current taxes or borrow it now and tax it later through future taxes?

Mr. HALL. Yeah, we certainly sort of constantly remind you that however you do it, whether you raise taxes or spending or etc., a lot of the stuff it depends on how you pay for it. Whether you let the deficit grow or not makes a big impact.

Mr. MCCLINTOCK. Well, the deficit is just a future tax. We borrow it now and we pay it back through future taxes. In other words, is not to borrow from the Clinton maxim, is not the spending stupid?

Mr. HALL. Well, certainly spending is the biggest single problem going forward. The rate of spending exceeds the tax rate.

Mr. MCCLINTOCK. Thank you.

Interim Chair BLACK. The gentleman's time has expired. The gentlelady from Washington. Ms. DelBene is now recognized for 5 minutes.

Ms. DELBENE. Thank you, Madam Chair and Director Hall. Thank you for being with us. My district in Washington State has a northern border and is also home to I am pretty sure nearly every point of view on every issue most of the time, but one key difference has been immigration reform. We have heard from business community, farmers, State-based community, folks in travel and tourism, law enforcement all asking for comprehensive immigration reform, and I was one of the folks who lead the bill that we introduced in the House in the 113th Congress similar to the one that passed the Senate that the CBO has said would have a significant impact in reducing the deficit about $700 billion in the second decade. I think you confirmed that was the correct number.

Mr. HALL. That sounds right.

Ms. DELBENE. But when we look at individual sectors, and when I was elected in talking to our farmers, they said we need two things. We need a farm bill and we need comprehensive immigration reform, and we got a farm bill and folks have said we are not sure we can stay in business if we do not have immigration reform. If you look at a sector like agriculture, do you see lack of immigration reform as actually having a negative impact on economic growth?

Mr. HALL. We have not done that sort of analysis. We would have to do a little work.

Ms. DELBENE. Well, I can tell you that farmers definitely feel that way, and it is an incredibly important issue, and the reckless executive order has not helped and has impacted many people's lives and has only continued to have a negative impact. Before coming to Congress, I was a business woman and entrepreneur and also ran the Department of Revenue for the State of Washington, and since coming to Congress, I have been very frustrated with our budget and appropriations process with how they do not work.

In particular, we seem to live off of continuing resolutions, and you would never run a business 30 or 60 days at a time, and you definitely, it is no way to budget. It is probably the most expensive and least efficient way to budget. But we also, with sequestration on top of that, we end up looking at folks have been focused on cuts but not on return on investment, and I know that sometimes spending money on important projects actually saves you money in the long run and we get a great return. I was wondering when you look at your models and look at things like infrastructure, research, and education, how does our lack of investment in those areas impact our future growth?

Mr. HALL. Well, I think the research is fairly clear that generally Federal investment does increase productivity and it does have an impact on growth. The research if pretty incomplete in that it, identifying the different kinds of investment is difficulty, what the rates of return are on different kinds of investment. One of the big things though about increasing investment is really depends upon how you pay for it. If you increase investment and reduce spending in another spot, so you do not have a net impact on spending, that is a much more positive impact on the economy than if you let a deficit grow.

Ms. DELBENE. But if we, for example, have a pothole in the road and we do not fix it and it might have cost a certain amount to fix that pothole, next time because we did not fix it, we end up having to replace the road bed, we end up spending a lot more because we did not make that investment early on. Is not that a fair point of view when we look at a lot of these issues that we are not funding, or providing those investments because we do not have a normal budget or appropriations process? Is not that hurting our ability to see progress in those areas?

Mr. HALL. That is right. Federal investment doing anything that sort of helps companies be more productive, move products around, encourage innovation, that does help productivity, and that is obviously one of our big problems going forward. In one of the issues, it is a little bit like in my mind a little bit like cutting taxes. They both can stimulate the economy and depends on how they work. They can both affect long-term growth. The question a little bit is how much? You know, investment, Federal investment in particular, there is often a big delay, and there is some impact on interest rates, and that impact on interest rates does raise the cost of debt in the economy. So, it is not quite so clear, for example, that if you just increase Federal investment, do not pay for it, let the deficit grow, that probably does not have a net positive on the economy.

Ms. DELBENE. But also just cutting and not investing in programs that give us a great return has a negative impact too, and I think that is our role to decide what is giving us a great return and making sure we are making those investments, seeing what is not working and not making those investments, and continuing resolutions and sequestration are us not taking that responsibility seriously here and not making those decisions and making the investments in the right way they need to be made. Thank you. My time has expired. I yield back, Madam Chair.

Interim Chair BLACK. The lady's time has expired. The gentleman from Ohio, Mr. Renacci, is recognized for 5 minutes.

Mr. RENACCI. Thank you, Madam Chairman. It is interesting. First, I want to go back to my colleague, Mr. Cole, and say the exact same thing. We could sit here all day and fire bullets back and forth on political issues, but that is not going to solve the issues of the day because the issue of the day is that we have to get a budget and we have to live with a budget, and before we can even get a budget we have to figure out where we are out which is another problem around here. I have mentioned since day one that we do not have a complete record of financial information because we do not allow for all of our debts to be added up, and we do not use the information that we have then to make decisions, and then we do not look at the past at the decisions we made.

As a business guy for 30 years, and actually a business guy that took over 60 failed businesses and successfully turned them around, you have to see where you are at first before you can go forward. So, my frustration always builds when we start to get into these political talking points because everybody's district is going to have issues that concern them.

My district, I can tell you, the businesses, the people, the individuals are all concerned about tax reform, regulation reform and Obamacare reform, so again it is not what the district is, it is what we can do as far as putting a budget together and getting things moving. But, Dr. Hall, do not we have the record revenues in the Treasury over the last few years?

Mr. HALL. That is right. Well, I am not sure the record. They are certainly above average right now and they are going to actually go up as a share of GDP. So, we do not have declining revenues.

Mr. RENACCI. Right. So, we have record revenues, and in my business world, what I would find is if you have record revenues you were really doing really well except when you had record expenditures that were exceeding those record revenues, and I heard you say earlier that one of our issues is that we are spending, you know, our biggest problem really is our spending problem. Would you agree?

Mr. HALL. Yes. That is the major contributor to the deficit.

Mr. RENACCI. So, until we come together as Republicans and Democrats and realize we have spending issues, and taxing, we are not going to tax our way out of this, and we can put a budget together, I think that is the starting point that I hope at some point this committee can get to, having a good solid budget that then we live with. My concern is again, it is extremely alarming that our interest and our national debt is projected to nearly quadruple to $768 billion in 2027. It appears that as numbers continue to grow, we are going to have less.

The time is now to start looking at our spending side because if we just sit back and start saying the last President was great, the President before that was great, and we do not do anything, we are going to be in a deeper, deeper hole in the next few years. Would you agree with that?

Mr. HALL. Absolutely. I think the sooner we get to solving the deficit problem whether it is spending or whether it is taxes or anything, but the sooner we start to address that, the less of a change it is going to be. The easier it is going to be to try to deal with it.

Mr. RENACCI. I think the sooner we recognize that it is one of the reasons I introduced the Fiscal State of the Nation which would require the Controller General would come before the House and Senate, a joint session of Congress, I had almost 170 cosponsors, Republicans and Democrats.

I actually hoped that new members here would join me as we have refiled that bill, but do you agree that it would be a good starting point to have someone, the Controller General, come before the House and Senate and explain our growing deficits and where the numbers are occurring and what is going on so we have a starting point?

Mr. HALL. Absolutely. I hope we were providing some of that information to you, but yes.

Mr. RENACCI. I understand, and that is what you are doing here today, but I think the important is as we continue to look at these numbers, we have to start to realize that the growth of our Federal debt is another issue concerns me and I heard one of my colleagues earlier talk about this. If we do nothing, I think the Federal deficit is projected to grow, if we just stay on the same track, $9.6 trillion in the next 10 years. Is that correct?

Mr. HALL. That is right.

Mr. RENACCI. So, these are all issues I hope that my colleagues on both sides of the aisle can start talking about as a way we can work together to come up with a solution and a budget. I also have another bill which I think is so important. When we pass a budget, we should follow a budget. We have had a Budget Act since 1974. Most people do not realize that even though we pass budgets, we never follow them.

Members from this committee, other committees come to the floor, pass bills that break the budget. If we are ever going to make things work, we have to come up with a solid budget and live with that budget and not break the budget. So, I am hoping that we can continue to work forward with these numbers. I appreciate the information. There is plenty of information in your report if everybody takes the time to read them. We are not going in a great direction. We do not have a healthy economy. We have what I would call a—we have an anemic economy. Would you agree with that?

Mr. HALL. Yes.

Mr. RENACCI. Thank you. I yield back.

Interim Chair BLACK. The gentleman's time has expired. The gentlelady from Florida, Ms. Wasserman Schultz, is now recognized for 5 minutes.

Ms. WASSERMAN SCHULTZ. Thank you, Madam Chair. Our colleagues on the other side of the aisle would do well to stop patting themselves on the back for and take credit for voters putting them in the majority rather than the cartographers and map drawers who did a really good job of partisan gerrymandering, Mr. McClintock, to ensure that the scales are tipped in favor in virtually every State. Particularly, the States where Republicans hold the majority and voters are not able to choose their legislatures but rather legislators choose their voters. And that is reflected in the brimming sea of diversity that we see in this committee on the other side of the aisle as opposed to our side of the aisle, and that also is reflective of the difference dramatically in the policies that result in how we govern. So, please spare us the political advice.

That having been said, I think it is important to note that Mr. Hall indicated that the slack in our economy is mainly attributed to the available labor force. Largely attributed as your said, Mr. Hall, to retirement of baby boomers and the stability of women in the workforce. Is that right?

Mr. HALL. That is right, and by stability, I mean that in the 1990s we had this great period of where women's labor force participation was growing very quickly and we had significantly more economic growth as a result and they have sort of closed that gap and it is now sort of holding, so we are no longer getting that faster growth.

Ms. WASSERMAN SCHULTZ. You did indicate in your opening statement that primarily, the slack in the economy is attributed to those two things.

Mr. HALL. Well, right, and really, I think I was trying to refer to the potential growth, the long-term growth of the economy, but yes, I did talk about those two things.

Ms. WASSERMAN SCHULTZ. Okay. Thank you. Our former CBO director, Douglas Elmendorf, in a recent talk noted that under the current caps on annual appropriations, Federal investment in infrastructure, R&D, education and training, will soon be smaller relative to GDP than at any time in the last 50 years. He said that is not forward-looking growth-oriented budget policy just to maintain the traditional level of investment as a percentage of the economy requires a substantial increase in the caps on appropriations. The caps on appropriations would you not agree are a large part of what limits our ability to see growth in the economy?

Mr. HALL. It certainly has been the limit on the discretionary spending growth. That has been part of why it looks to be declining over the next 10 years.

Ms. WASSERMAN SCHULTZ. With the Budget Control Act of 2011 and sequestration, we continue to see dramatic cuts in nondefense discretionary spending, dramatic cuts.

In 2010, nondefense discretionary spending was 4.5 percent of GDP, 2016 it was 3 percent. It is projected that in 2027 nondefense discretionary spending will only be 2.4 percent of GDP, and furthermore investment in infrastructure as a percent of GDP has dropped from 0.8 percent in 1980 to 0.5 percent in 2015. Investment in research has dropped from 1 percent in 1965 to 0.4 percent of GDP in 2013, and finally investment for education and training programs has dropped from 1 percent of GDP in 1975 to 0.5 percent in 2013.

Director Hall, do you agree with your predecessor that capping investing in research, infrastructure, and education is incompatible with a budget policy that promotes growth in the American economy? And should not we aim each year to include a certain percentage of spending on discretionary programs that promote economic growth especially given the President's Muslim ban which will among other things keep those leaders and research and development out of our country and hurt our economy?

Mr. HALL. I would not make a recommendation, but I will say that increase in Federal investment is one of the tools you have for increasing potential GDP growth because it does increase productivity of labor going forward.

Ms. WASSERMAN SCHULTZ. And would not you say that generally taking a balanced approach which is what Democrats have promoted over the last 8 years to responsible spending cuts and generating revenue is the most responsible way to address deficits over a period of time, and would not you also say then when it comes to dealing with our debt, that there is a dramatically negative impact on our overall economy when we threaten, as a Congress, to potentially not pay our bills?

Mr. HALL. I should say however Congress decides to address the deficit, if they address it in a broader fashion, they may need to make less dramatic changes in any one thing so that does seem like that is a strategy certainly Congress could take.

Ms. WASSERMAN SCHULTZ. Thank you, very much. I yield back the balance of my time.

Interim Chair BLACK. The gentlelady yields back. The gentleman from Minnesota. Mr. Lewis is recognized for 5 minutes.

Mr. LEWIS. Thank you, Madam Chair, and thank you, Dr. Hall, for being here today. Talk a little bit about Federal investment or Federal spending. In 2002, the Federal budget was $2 trillion. Today, it is $3.4 trillion to your numbers. The 50-year average is about 18.4 percent of revenues. We are well above that now and headed above that. Outlays, however, are well above the 50-year average as well. Correct?

Mr. HALL. That is correct.

Mr. LEWIS. The top one percent of income earners, if we are going to look at revenues to balance this budget, the top one percent of income earners right now pay about $543 billion in income taxes. That is less than this year's deficit. Correct?

Mr. HALL. I think that is right. I do not know the numbers exactly but that sounds about right.

Mr. LEWIS. My question is this, I do not think we have a revenue problem, if you look at these numbers again we are above the 50-year average of 18.4 percent and moving higher than that. How would we do that if you are just going to raise revenue? I mean there is not enough money at the top is there?

Mr. HALL. Yes, we have not had any real specific analysis of that but you are right, putting it all in revenues makes it a pretty significant revenue increase just like putting it all in outlays involves a pretty dramatic outlay drop. So, sort of spreading it out is a different sort of strategy.

Mr. LEWIS. You are servicing the debt and that interest on the debt, $768 billion larger than the defense budget, for instance, I believe in the next 10 years. What are you basing that on with regards to interest rates? I think the post-World War II 10-year treasury average is about 5.7 percent or down, way down now to about 2.4 percent. How did you come up with that calculation?

Mr. HALL. First of all, interest rates have been really low. We have interest rates climbing up into somewhat their historical range but we are still kind of at the lower end of that range. So, we are somewhere over 3 percent eventually on the interest rates. And that is a really important point to be honest, because we are at a pretty low interest rate relative to history and, in fact, if interest rates go up by more——

Mr. LEWIS. Or back to their average.

Mr. HALL. Or back to their average. Let me give you an example; if interest rates were one percentage point higher over this 10-year period than our projection, we are talking about adding $1.6 trillion to the debt over that time period. And that is a lot of money for just one percentage point. So, that is one of the more important things in our forecast.

Mr. LEWIS. So, the debt interest payment of $768 billion in 10 years is based on historically low interest rates?

Mr. HALL. That is correct.

Mr. LEWIS. Let's talk a little bit about Japan. I am not an expert on their immigration policy, but I do not know that it has changed remarkably. But I do know their economy has hit this deflationary spiral. So I am not certain if you got the same policy in one particular area but all of sudden you go into a tailspin that you can blame that policy. But what you might be able to look at is credit expansion. And we have had a very similar experience here where we have monetized a lot of debt, where we have let the credit expansion go, created asset bubbles, as some would say, on the monetary side.

Is it your experience, or I do not want to ask your opinion, but your analysis that Japan is suffering a debt lag? That we have created so much debt that they cannot grow their way out and is that a danger for America as far as a hyperinflation scenario stuck in a debt spiral and stuck with deflation and low growth?

Mr. HALL. I am afraid I do not know enough about Japan or Japan's policies.

Mr. LEWIS. That makes two of us.

Mr. HALL. Okay, so it would be hard. And we can follow up with some description, if you like, on Japan and what has been happening there.

Mr. LEWIS. I mean, there is a reason for these low growth rates. And, you know, we have created money, we have created fiat money, we have certainly engaged in Federal spending. We look at those figures I just cited, well above historical means, so why the low growth rates?

Mr. HALL. Again, I do not know enough about Japan to offer an opinion.

Mr. LEWIS. I would suggest that the reason we have not hit 3 percent growth for 11 straight quarters, the reason that during the Reagan robust recovery, even the Clinton robust recovery where we had growth of 5, 6, 7 percent is the level of debt today, that we are stuck. Our balance sheets do not look so good, and when you are trying to service that kind of debt it is very hard to grow out of it.

Mr. HALL. Yeah, I will just say one of the most remarkable things that is going on now, and has since the end of the recession, has been very low productivity growth of 0.8 percent. And we do not understand that very well. And that has been a major head wind.

Mr. LEWIS. One final point quickly, Dr. Hall, and thanks again for coming. But, when we fund Federal investment, where does that money come from? Some of it comes out of the private sector, some of that which would be private investment correct?

Mr. HALL. That is correct.

Mr. LEWIS. Thank you, sir, I yield back my time.

Interim Chair BLACK. The gentleman's time is expired. The Gentleman from New York, Mr. Higgins is recognized for 5 minutes.

Mr. HIGGINS. Thank you, Madam Chair. I am listening to the discussion here which is thoughtful, and I believe that people truly are sincere in their beliefs about the performance of the American economy and the policies that we in Congress are responsible for enacting to help influence hopefully economic growth. And I think there are two very different views of it.

You know, the good thing about the economy is, you know policy either works or it does not. It is not ideological; it is arithmetical. And if you look at the performance under various administrations relative to the policies they advance, the measure of their effectiveness or lack of effectiveness is the performance of the economy.

Now, it has been referenced here that in the waning days of the last Bush administration a decision was made to enact tax cuts that disproportionately benefited higher wage earners, people that make a lot of money. The theory is trickle down, it is supply side, it is call it what you will it is because if they save money because of tax policy, that money will find its way back into the economy in new business investment and job growth. That is the theory. That is indisputable. That is what they say.

Job growth during the George W. Bush administration was the lowest level in the past 75 years. In the waning days, the economy went into a very severe contraction. In March of 2009, the stock market was at 5,600. We were losing 600,000 jobs a month. The auto industry was a disaster. The U.S. and world financial markets were falling apart. Something had to be done.

So, new policies were put in place to allow those tax cuts for the very, very wealthy to expire and continue tax cuts for the middle class because higher wages, higher take home pay increases aggregate demand in the economy, aggregate demand creates economic growth. And as a result, since 2010, in the past 6 years, we created in this economy almost 16 million private sector jobs.

You know, the American economy we used to make things and sell them to the rest of the world, now the things that we used to make and sell to the rest of the world they make and sell to us.

As a consequence, 70 percent of the American economy is consumption.

So, how do you create aggregate demand in the economy? You put more money in the pockets of more Americans as humanly possible because here is what you know, they are going to spend it. And when they spend it, there is growth. I think, you know, you are always looking for silver linings in these views of economic policy. And I think the one real clear silver lining here is infrastructure spending. And there is talk about a trillion-dollar bill, and it does two things. In the immediate sense, it creates jobs, I think 43 jobs for every million dollars of investment in the construction trades and supply and materials industry.

But the second economic benefit you get from that is, when you invest in infrastructure, it unleashes the creativity and the resources of the private sector. So, your views on a trillion-dollar investments in infrastructure publicly financed. And do not tell me about deficit financing because this Nation spent $110 billion rebuilding the roads and bridges of Afghanistan. This Government spent $76 billion rebuilding the roads and bridges of Iraq, both of which were deficit financed and did not create one American job. So, your views on infrastructure investment and financed in a traditional way.

Interim Chair BLACK. Mr. Hall, you have 10 seconds to answer this. And I am afraid, Mr. Higgins, since you did not leave him adequate time, I am going to let him give a very brief comment, but if Members would remember if they are asking a question and they need to leave a little time for our witness to answer the question. Otherwise if you could briefly answer and if there is more that you would like to do if you could do it in writing.

Mr. HALL. Okay. A basic principle I think is all over our work. You know whether you change spending or change taxes, if you increase spending or lower tax, however. How you pay for that makes a difference because the deficit has an impact on that. So if you increase spending but you do not pay for it you increase the deficit, that makes a difference, how you pay for things. So that is something just to consider always with what we are talking about.

Interim Chair BLACK. Thank you, Mr. Hall. The Gentleman from Texas, Mr. Arrington, is recognized for 5 minutes.

Mr. ARRINGTON. Thank you Madam Chair and Dr. Hall, I appreciate your time and your service and I am happy to be on this bipartisan House Budget Committee, I say that a little tongue and cheek based on some of the comments that are made. The American people are tired of partisan bickering and tit-for-tat. They want us to do like they do in their businesses and in their homes and their daily lives and roll up our sleeves and go to work and solve this problem.

The other thing they are tired of is Congress playing by a different set of rules. And one of the rules that they have to play by and live by is that they have to live within our means. And so, we have to work together to solve this. I am excited to be on this committee because I think it is the greatest threat to the future of our country.

My commitment is not to the Republican Party or to the leadership, my commitment is to my three children that they will have a safe, strong and free America to live in. That they will in fact have a future to grow up in the shining city on a Hill, and this is the greatest threat to that future. And so, I am grateful to be a part of the problem-solving venture that we are about to undertake.

I think there is spending issues and cuts to be made across the board, but I am very concerned about the elephant in the room that was mentioned. That mandatory spending and the entitlement programs that were mentioned are squeezing very important investment that we need to make as a country if we are going to have a prosperous Nation going forward. Now, I think about agriculture.

AG is the lifeblood of economy in west Texas and if we do not make the investment in risk management tools for our farmers or the safety net, we will not have the capacity to feed and clothe the American people. Dr. Hall, how much do we spend on the AG risk management or the AG programs within the farm bill as a percentage of our Federal budget?

Mr. HALL. I do not know, but it is not a large percentage.

Mr. ARRINGTON. A quarter of 1 percent, so that we have a safe and affordable and abundant supply of food for the American people. We have cut billions of dollars in that discretionary program. Whether it is transportation and making sure that we meet the transportation needs or R&Ds so that we are the laboratory of innovation for the world and we continue to be on the cutting edge of technology in this country. Or it is on National Defense.

I am concerned on the lack of investment in these important areas all because we have squeezed I think just about all of the blood out of the turnip on the discretionary side. At what point Dr. Hall do we reach diminishing returns on the cuts on the discretionary side, maybe in some of the programs I have mentioned?

Mr. HALL. It is hard to say on any of this. You know the growing deficit, any of these numbers, they look bad and we have been on record to say that the debt is unsustainable if you look out a lot of years, so it is hard to say too much. Focus on discretionary spending, one of the things I think is a little interesting sobering factoid here, is we expect in 10 years that just the payment on debt, the net interest on debt, will exceed all non-defense discretionary spending in the country. So, that will become a bigger item in all non-defense discretionary spending, that is part of the problem. You have this net interest becoming a major part in the budget going forward.

Mr. ARRINGTON. Quick response; of the risks to balancing our budget and getting our arms around this deficit spending and national debt, which one is the greatest risk, interest rates, economic growth, domestic spending or the entitlement programs and the runaway costs there?

Mr. HALL. It is hard to rank them, right, because obviously you can look at any of those to address the deficit problem.

Mr. ARRINGTON. Here is my last point and again, thank you for your time. We cannot keep kicking the can down the road, we do not have any more runway. We do not need more analysis; we do not need more accountants or budgetary experts. We need leaders with the courage to solve the problem. The problem is mandatory spending. I look forward to getting after it, as we say in West Texas. Madam Chair, I yield back.

Interim Chair BLACK. The gentleman's time is expired. The gentleman from California, Mr. Khanna, is recognized for 5 minutes.

Mr. KHANNA. Thank you, Madam Chair. I appreciate following Congressman Arrington. We may not agree with much regarding economics but he has shown a lot of graciousness in reaching out to the freshman class across the aisle and trying to build stability in the country first so I appreciate following him. Dr. Hall, thank you for your service, and your service not just in this role but at the Commerce Department and Treasury Department and White House and I look forward to hearing some of your expertise.

I represent a district at the heart of Silicon Valley with Google, Apple, Yahoo, Intel, Cisco and Enrico Moretti, economist at Berkeley, has written that there is a tech multiplier of 4.5 jobs. For every one job created in tech, four and a half jobs are created. Pastor Trieber and Pastor Burnell who are in for the National Prayer Breakfast will tell you that in our district not everyone who works for tech goes to their church but there are folks that are baristas, and lawyers and others who have those jobs partly because of the tech industry.

Now in Eastern Kentucky, thanks in part to Ranking Member Yarmuth's work with the administration, there was this model where 40 jobs were recently created for folks of coal-miners' kids who were being trained on IOS software on the Apple phone and android software with the Google phone, a four month class. All of them have jobs. It was funded by the tech initiative that the administration worked on with Congress and the Regional Appalachian Economic Center. My issue, and I do not think it is a partisan issue, is how do we get these tech jobs across the country and what are your thoughts on what this congress needs to do to make that possible?

Mr. HALL. It is a little hard to speak too specific to that, I do not want to make specific recommendations, that is not what CBO does. But I can put it in general terms, the long run problems are, you know we talked a little bit about the labor force participation. Getting the labor force growth increase, working age people sort of back in the labor force but also there is productivity side of things.

There are lots of things that government can consider that will increase private sector productivity, right? Whether it is looking at tax policy, where trying to find a more efficient way of collecting taxes that is hopefully tax neutral. Whether it is looking at the regulatory environment, whether it is looking at increased Federal investment.

All those things are things that can impact private sector productivity, and that is really an important part of the recipe. One of the real difficulties we have, anybody has right now, on being too specific, we do not understand productivity growth really well and we do not understand how policies affect productivity growth very well. So, it is very hard for almost anybody to have too many solid recommendations about how to achieve higher productivity because we just do not know that much about it.

Mr. KHANNA. I appreciate that, would you say that preparing folks for these jobs though has to be a component of it?

Mr. HALL. Yes, absolutely.

Mr. KHANNA. The other line of questioning I have is slightly different and that is on Social Security and without taking a particular view. If we were to scrap the cap, how much revenue would that raise? And how much would that go towards solving some of the structural deficits?

Mr. HALL. It would certainly have an impact. I do not have the number in my head. But we actually did that calculation and that options for reducing the deficit volume that we just produced, that was one of the options that we put in there. If you look at that, and we can follow up too, that will give you an idea of how much of an impact that would have.

Mr. KHANNA. I would appreciate that, I yield back the balance of my time.

Interim Chair BLACK. The gentleman yields back, we appreciate that balance of time. The gentleman from South Carolina, Mr. Sanford, is recognized for 5 minutes.

Mr. SANFORD. Thank you, and I appreciate the thoughtful comments from my colleagues from New York and from California, and we do see things differently. And I want to bore down though on what my other colleague from California, Mr. McClintock was getting at. In the danger of a sovereign debt crisis, I think it is much more real than what people realize and I think it is much closer than people realize. So, you yourself have identified the debt as unsustainable, that we are on a path that we cannot possibly continue. And I think the numbers are compelling on that case.

But what I would like to flesh out is how this may be a nearer term event that would have cataclysmic consequences with regard to the value of our currency with regard to future inflation with regard to the American standard of living. I think it is interesting, I saw a McKinsey report the other day and what it showed was, we are at about 250 percent debt to GDB globally and in the wake of 2008 what we saw was a roughly $57 trillion increase in debt which was highly unusual because what the report showed was that going back really over the last 50 plus years, actually no it was more than that, it went back to 1930. That in the wake of financial crisis or economic slowdown, that historically there was a de-leveraging that followed.

But in this instance, post-2008, what we have seen is a reverse, is significant leveraging in the wake of a financial crises. And therefore we lived in a time like no other, and you can see the same numbers at the Federal level, you know our debt to GDP numbers, I guess a post-World War II high, and they are at a peace time high. So, I was looking at the numbers the other day and I think this is a really interesting chart, that again suggests how vulnerable we are and how a crisis could come much sooner than people realize.

This is from the Fed, and it's net worth as a percentage of disposable income, you could also do net worth as a percentage of GDP. But basically, what it shows is over the last 75 years, we have been fairly constant at an average of around 500 percent of net worth to disposable income. But in the early, I guess late 1990s, we had a peak it represented the tech bubble, we went above 600 percent and we did it again in the housing crisis, or just pre-housing crisis went above 600 percent and we have done it again now.

And what is interesting what followed the tech bubble we know, what followed the housing bubble we know, but we are at that same percentage in an overall inflated environment with regard to debt both domestic and internationally. Is there a much greater level of vulnerability than we realize? And let me add one other thought to that. I pulled the numbers on economic expansions, we are now living in the fourth longest economic expansion in American history. So, we had the tech bubble, we had the Reagan expansion, we had the Kennedy-Johnson expansions but you know the average is 60 months we are about a third past that which would suggest to me another layer of vulnerability. And finally, we live in a zero interest rate policy. Which is a policy that we have in essence never lived in.

You know, I guess it was Roosevelt's Treasury secretary that at time of the Depression talked about pushing on a string how there was just no more juice in terms of making things happen. So, would you flush out in the minute and a half that I guess you have, with a little bit of color with regard to, you know, while we may be unsustainable in the long run, maybe this can creep up on us much sooner than people realize?

Mr. HALL. Sure. Part of the trouble is that there just is not research, and there is no way to know how much debt is too much.

Mr. SANFORD. Well, I think there is regression to the mean for a reason. I mean, I think it is even dangerous when we talk about interest policy and we say, Well, we are going back to the average. Well that is not what has historically happened, the reason you regress to the mean is typically you go far on the other side so interest rates go up a bunch to give you that average. So, I think that the law of averages and numbers works.

Mr. HALL. Yeah, and the sort of comparison that we wind up making and it probably should be a sobering comparison, 77 percent of GDP and debt is a really high number. You go up a little bit more and you have the highest debt ratio since the end of World War II. The end of World War II was a pretty special time, so it is way above historical numbers.

Mr. SANFORD. Well, and that was a case where we were actually fighting for our survival as a republic. Right now, that money is in essence going towards consumption and again what many would argue to be sustainability. Oh, we are going to have fun, come on.

Interim Chair BLACK. The gentleman's time is expired, I am very sorry. The ranking member, Mr. Yarmuth, is recognized.

Mr. YARMUTH. Thank you, Madam Chairman. Once again, thank you, Director Hall. I look forward to reading your new publication. I think that would be something mandatory reading for all of us here. One thing we have not talked about yet during this hearing is tax expenditures. And I think your report shows that tax expenditures actually are on a path, if not now, they are larger than the discretionary spending in total, including defense spending. Somewhere going to $1.5 trillion. Is there any difference, in terms of the impact on the budget, between a dollar of tax expenditure and a dollar of discretionary spending?

Mr. HALL. No, the effect on the deficit is the same.

Mr. YARMUTH. And have you done an analysis of what types of discretionary spending maybe have a more positive or negative impact on the budget as on the deficit as you would have . . . so, you would for instance, a charitable deduction versus R&D tax credits versus mortgage deductions.

Mr. HALL. Not that comes to my mind so much. Our colleagues at the Joint Committee on Taxation who have done a lot more of that work they might have some numbers for you.

Mr. YARMUTH. And last year, this House renewed about $800 billion of tax expenditures as I recall with no offset [inaudible].

Mr. HALL. The numbers, that could be correct.

Mr. YARMUTH. It was pretty substantial.

Mr. HALL. Yes it was.

Mr. YARMUTH. So, what we are talking about, and I hope you dealt with this in the new publication, because clearly when you are looking at over a trillion dollars of tax expenditures, you are looking at another significant impact on the deficit. And something that we do not spend nearly enough time looking at in terms of which ones really pay off for the taxpayers. I mean, most of the mortgage deduction benefit goes to wealthier tax payers, is that not correct?

Mr. HALL. I think that is probably correct. Can I just say something in general, I referred to it but one of the ways to try to approve efficiency and productivity is to look at the efficiency of taxes, of our tax system. Right? Because our tax system has lots of things that encourage behavior that causes distortions. And so there are things one can look at.

Reducing taxes on capital investment for example—it is a really direct way of affecting productivity because capital investment increases productivity. Worrying about our tax base, right? There is some offshoring behavior that reduces our tax base. Some of those things, especially if they are sort of tax neutral, would have an impact potentially on long-term growth without adding to the deficit.

Mr. YARMUTH. Well, presumably, we are going to have that debate later this year as the House takes on tax reform. So that will be an interesting forum. I know this will be totally out of character for me. I am going to ask questions that have no political point at all. I am just curious about them. In your report, you project Medicare spending per beneficiary to go up 4.3 percent through 2027, which is 3 percent higher than it has been over the last 5 years. Why such a dramatic increase in projection of the cost per beneficiary?

Mr. HALL. That one is actually pretty difficult for us to forecast. Healthcare spending has been consistently growing faster than GDP. And a lot of that for us is just continuing the trend that we have seen in that. And it is actually part of our forecast that will continue, per beneficiary growth of health care generally, will grow faster than GDP. And that actually is part of the growing deficit.

Mr. YARMUTH. But that has not been the case over the last 5 years.

Mr. HALL. Right.

Mr. YARMUTH. Part of it is the ACA, part of it is in the economy and so forth. I know there are a lot of actors there. My point being that could be a dramatic difference in your long-term forecast for

Medicare. If the growth rates per beneficiary stayed at one third of what you are projecting.

Mr. HALL. Well, that is right that could have an impact. And you are right that the growth has slowed down. And I do not know if we have it in this report but somewhere we have got a sensitivity analysis where we vary the cost of health care to see what sort of impact that has on the budget deficit. We can get back to you on that.

Mr. YARMUTH. Thanks. Another point you make is that the subsidies on the exchanges, assuming that they are not repealed, would double basically from this year until 10 years. I was curious whether that was predicated on doubling the number of insureds. A rise in the premiums so the subsidies have to keep pace with the premiums under current law. Is that the reason it would double in 10 years or is it a combination of both?

Mr. HALL. It is probably both, but certainly, I would think most of it is the increased use of the exchange and increased use of the expansion so I think they are both in there.

Mr. YARMUTH. Okay, so now turn to Medicaid. This is now regular Medicaid not the expanding Medicaid, you project expenditures growing from $389 billion in 2017 to $650 billion in 2027 which is a significant increase. I do not know what it is, 70 percent growth over that period of time, but it's 5.5 percent a year growth.

Is that because you are projecting, again rising cost per beneficiaries or because you expect that more people to be involved and be eligible for Medicaid? Which would reflect a really bad economy. Or would it be because such a huge percentage of Medicaid is used for skilled nursing and you expect the senior population to eat up a larger chunk of the Medicaid budget?

Mr. HALL. Yeah, to get to that level of detail I have to get back to you. I am pretty sure a big chunk of that is simply the increased number of people but we can break that out for you.

Mr. YARMUTH. Okay, but would that be on the skilled nursing side because to say that the population eligible for Medicaid is going to grow that much over the next 5 years, again indicates an economy that is going in the tank which does not comport with the rest of your forecast.

Mr. HALL. Right, I mean we have pretty modest growth, but one of the things we do have is a continuing trend and faster growth in income for high income folks so the distribution of income, we have that continuing to change and that is a trend going forward that is been there for a while.

Mr. YARMUTH. And now going to Medicaid expansion, your projection is that between now and 2027, the number of people and the expanded Medicaid would go from 12 million to 17 million people.

Mr. HALL. Right.

Mr. YARMUTH. And that the total expense of expanded Medicaid would go from $70 billion to $142 billion, so that is 100 percent increase, 7 percent a year is what you are projecting? Again, I am curious to why that is such a huge increase.

Mr. HALL. That one I know.

Mr. YARMUTH. Okay, good.

Mr. HALL. Right now, there are 31 States and D.C. that have expanded and that is about 50 percent of the eligible people. We expect that the increase, the number of States that adopt Medicaid expansion, that will increase about 70 percent of the total people of all the States. So, it is from growing State acceptance of that.

Mr. YARMUTH. Okay, good answer. Wish we could see that. Policy does not look like it is going in that direction, however. You know in my State we have, I think arguably the most successful expansion of Medicaid in the country. We do start insured by more than 60 percent and in my district now we are at 3 percent on insured, 81,000 on expanded Medicaid.

And the projections if, not your projections, but other projections, show that if we actually were to rescind the Affordable Care Act, the Medicaid expansion or just the Medicaid expansion we would lose an awful lot of jobs, 10s of thousands of jobs in Kentucky; one estimate—44,000 jobs and $30 billion worth of economic activity over the next 5 years. Does your data, your analysis of the Affordable Care Act reflect that kind of potential loss in economic activity and employment in other areas of the country or across the country?

Mr. HALL. I am not sure if we have that level of detail. The main impact of, for example ACA repeal, is a change in labor supply. We think that would be an increase in labor supply that would sort of increase the economic growth from and that would sort of counter some of the effects. That level of detail, I do not know offhand what we have thought about that.

Mr. YARMUTH. Well, thank you very much once again for your testimony. I yield back.

Interim Chair BLACK. The gentleman's time has expired. The gentleman from Pennsylvania, Mr. Smucker, is recognized for 5 minutes.

Mr. SMUCKER. Thank you, Madam Chair. Good morning, Dr. Hall.

Mr. HALL. Good morning.

Mr. SMUCKER. Thanks for being here. As any other freshman here, and probably other members as well, we have just come through a campaign where, I know I have had many, many conversations with people throughout my district and heard concerns that they have expressed. And one of the top things that we have heard is people believe that the economy is not working for them as it should. They are concerned that their kids, their grandkids, will not have the same opportunities to live the American dream that we all have had. People are very concerned about that. And they are concerned that we are asking future generations to pay the bill. And is it not true, Dr. Hall, that is what we are doing? If we cannot solve this problem here, we are transferring that problem to future generations.

Mr. HALL. I think that is a fair statement. We do have a literature. It is a little research talking about the intergenerational effects of the debt that we can get to you. But I think that is a concern.

Mr. SMUCKER. So, that is one concern. People are also very concerned; their perception is that their elected leaders are not willing to make the tough decisions to solve the problems that we are faced with. And I am hoping that we are about to change that. And I am pleased to be on the Budget Committee to work to try to solve some of these difficult issues.

And I agree with many of the other comments that have been said here today; this is not a partisan issue. These are issues that we should be looking to try to find solutions. It will take us working across the aisle to move our country in the right direction. So I am hoping that this is the beginning to finding some of these solutions.

The other thing that I have heard and I am going to get another question to you, you know I am Pennsylvania, Lancaster, Pennsylvania, a lot of entrepreneurs, small companies that have grown, developed in technology or whatever it might be and created jobs.

And the business owners that I talked to today believe that it is more difficult and as a business owner myself I have seen this myself, it is more difficult, there is less incentive to invest additional capital into new technologies, to hire people because of the environment that we have created this economy. They believe the regulatory environment holds them back, holds individuals, holds businesses back. Prevents that kind of economic growth that we have seen before. They believe the tax policy is no longer working for them. Do you think we are seeing that kind of impact?

Mr. HALL. I certainly think that that is a potential area for improving the long-term growth, right? Because one of the two big challenges is productivity. You need some regulation, eliminating some regulation can actually hurt productivity but having regulation that is unnecessary or goes too far can impact productivity. Tax policies can impact productivity.

Mr. SMUCKER. We have talked about whether we need to tax our way out of this—whether we need to cut spending. I think we also need to look at establishing the right environment to encourage capital investment, to encourage more hiring, to encourage activities by individuals and business to create that economic growth. I think it has been done before. But my question to you in this regard is how much impact will that have? Say for instance we are able to get to a 3 percent or 4 percent annual growth.

You know the numbers I am looking at look every bit as bad and worse, they do not look any better from this side of the table than they do before. But how much impact could we have if we create an environment for much stronger economic growth?

Mr. HALL. The problem is so big, you cannot do it with just economic growth, I think.

Mr. SMUCKER. Can you give a sense though on how much of a difference that would make?

Mr. HALL. Well, right now, we think that productivity is going to grow to about 1.3 percent a year by the end of our 10-year period. In the 1990s it was as high as 2 percent, which is very unusual. Well let's say we got another half percentage point of productivity. In 10 years, we are talking about having a deficit of about $50 billion lower. So, the deficit going from 1.4 to .9, that is an impact but it is not balanced and we still have the continuing worsening demographics going forward.

Mr. SMUCKER. Thank you, Madam Chair, my time has expired.

Interim Chair BLACK. The gentleman's time has expired. And I now recognize Mr. Faso, from New York, for 5 minutes.

Mr. FASO. Thank you, Madam Chair. Dr. Hall, thank you. You raise productivity, how much would making permanent the 179-tax incentive for business investments or 100 percent expensing for capital expenditures, how much have you factored that into or done an analysis as to how much that could improve productivity?

Mr. HALL. I do not know if we have done an analysis on that. We assume that they expire when they expire. So, I would have to see if we have done an exercise like that.

Mr. FASO. Could you get back to us on that?

Mr. HALL. Sure.

Mr. FASO. And I am also a member of the Agriculture Committee and I was appointed to the Nutrition Sub-Committee, and I have noted that despite the general improvement in the economy in terms of employment, that we still have not seen a decline in recipients under SNAP. And I am wondering if you have factored in and looked at that factor as well?

Mr. HALL. That is sort of part of our forecast and we do think there is still slack in the economy. But the underlying forecast on SNAP I think does incorporate our economic forecast. We think we are still about one and one half million jobs short of full employment right now even though the unemployment rate is very low, so that is still a significant slack left.

Mr. FASO. And I would add some of the comments of my colleagues, one of the things I heard frequently on the campaign trail and speaking to business was that they have jobs, they just cannot find qualified people to fill the jobs. And often these are jobs that might have technical skills, they might need some basic mechanical skills and training in robotics etcetera.

I am thinking of one particular school, near my district, Hudson Valley Community College where the guy who runs it, is a robotic training facility, he has about 150 students in it every year. Every single student has a job. He told me that you could have literally 50 of his type centers around the country, and you still would not meet the need for employment of those kind of jobs. Any comment on that?

Mr. HALL. Two things come to mind, our issue with slowly growing labor force, that is not going as quickly. Part of that is, working age people are not entering the labor force like they have in the past, so the participation rates of working age rates are really lower now than they have been in the past. That is a puzzle and we think a lot of that just does not look like it is coming back, so that is something that maybe is important here.

And the second is, you know, one of the things that we have done a little work on is some Federal investment in things like education and training. And, in fact we are coming out very shortly on a blog on the affects about what we see is the evidence on the effects of education and training that going forward that might address that issue.

Mr. FASO. Okay, I would be interested in seeing that. I am also interested in seeing that publication you referenced about the 100 best ways we could use to reduce the deficit. Speaking of the debt, what did you say our 10-year growth in national debt is going to be?

Mr. HALL. We are going to hit about 89 percent of GDP.

Mr. FASO. And in terms of actual amount of debt, it is going to go from, right now we are at about $19 trillion to?

Mr. HALL. I think it's $30 trillion.

Mr. FASO. Ten-trillion dollar increase in the debt over 10 years, does it get a little frustrating coming up here to Congress and to tell us and the American people that their national debt is going to be $30 trillion in 10 years, and no one seems to pay attention?

Mr. HALL. One of things I notice every year when we put out this report, we do a little press conference or we talk to press and let them ask questions, and one of the question is always "What is new about this report?" And the most notable thing to me is well, it still has the same punch line and a year ago, debt is large and it is growing and at some points it is unsustainable. That is a continuing message from CBO and it has been that message for quite a while.

Well Dr. Hall thank you for your service. I would not recommend it but maybe you need to set your hair on fire when you are giving that presentation, maybe they would pay attention then. Thank you so much. I yield back to Madam Chairman.

Interim Chair BLACK. The gentleman yields back time. Thank you very much. The gentleman from Ohio, Mr. Johnson, is recognized for 5 minutes.

Mr. JOHNSON. Thank you Madam Chair, and thank you Dr. Hall for joining us today. Let me turn to direct spending or mandatory spending. You know, when I was first elected in 2010, the first phone call I got was from my nearly 80-year-old mother, and it was not to say congratulations it was to say, "All right, son, what are you going to do to make sure Washington protects my Social Security benefits because if they do not, I am coming to live with you." The next phone call I got was from my wife who said "You better do what your mother said."

For many years after the 1983 Social Security reforms, the Social Security trust fund ran fairly large surpluses. This was done deliberately to try to ensure the trust fund would have resources to pay benefits for a long time. So, what is the current cash flow situation with Social Security?

Mr. HALL. Right now, their outlays exceed the revenues, even excluding interest by a fair amount. This year the outlays will exceed revenues by about $55 billion.

Mr. JOHNSON. Wow. How long do you think Social Security will last at that rate?

Mr. HALL. Right now, we have our exhaustion date at 2030.

Mr. JOHNSON. Okay. If Social Security continues to pay out more in benefits than it collects in taxes, what, in your opinion, will that mean for current beneficiaries if we do not take any action here? I can guess what that is, I can kind of put the two and two of what you just said together, but I would like to hear it from you on the record.

Mr. HALL. Actually, our assumptions in this is that the beneficiaries will still continue to get what they are promised. So, even though, unless Congress acts, beneficiaries will not get their full outlays, we assume that that happens. If they did not, in 2030, benefits would just have to be reduced by about 29 percent right away.

Mr. JOHNSON. All right. So, is it true the longer Congress waits to reform Social Security, the harder it is to implement the reforms without affecting current retirees?

Mr. HALL. It is.

Mr. JOHNSON. Okay. Let me go back and talk a little bit about economic growth. You know in a 2015 study on repealing the Affordable Care Act, the Congressional Budget Office determined that repeal would increase GDP by about 0.7 percent on average over the median term, that is 2021 through 2025. Mostly, by repealing the provisions that are expected to reduce the supply of labor in the economy. So, how would repealing the Affordable Care Act affect the expected supply of labor in the economy? Would it lead to an overall benefit in the economy in your view?

Mr. HALL. Repealing it would likely increase the supply of labor in the economy, not quite 1 percentage point and actually would give a boost to GDP growth because of that increase in labor supply, our latest estimate was about 0.7 percent on GDP.

Mr. JOHNSON. Okay so if we were to repeal, it would increase the GDP by about 0.7 and the expected supply of labor, tell me again what that would go to.

Mr. HALL. Sure, we think that the number of people that would increase their hours or re-enter the labor force that would increase by 0.8, 0.9 percent of the labor force. That would be the boost to the labor force.

Mr. JOHNSON. I am asking you to do some mental math here, I know that, but at the current labor rate that we are experiencing, you got any idea of how many millions of people that would be that would be back in the labor force.

Mr. HALL. Right. I do not off hand. I do not want to guess.

Mr. JOHNSON. Can you take that as a question please?

Mr. HALL. We can do that pretty quickly, somebody just needs to look it up for me.

Mr. JOHNSON. Yeah, I need a calculator too, I am sorry. So, thanks a lot, I appreciate you answering my questions. Madam Chair, I yield back.

Interim Chair BLACK. The gentleman yields back. I do want to reference the report that did come from CBO, Budgetary and Economic Effects of Repealing the Affordable Care Act and I will read a line from this, in addition to the questioning by the Gentleman from Ohio. And the paragraph begins with "The Macroeconomic feedback effects of repealing the ACA would lower the Federal Deficit by $216 billion on the period from 2016 to 2025." So, it would have a significant economic affect in lowering. The gentleman from Georgia, Mr. Ferguson is recognized for 5 minutes.

Mr. FERGUSON. Thank you, Madam Chairman. Dr. Hall, thank you for coming today. I guess one of the joys of being a freshman and going late in this game is I have gotten to hear a lot of these comments and have learned an awful lot.

So, a couple questions for you. First of all, do you believe that the rules set by Congress that you have to follow for scoring the budget and the policy changes do they allow us to accurately look in the future. Just a yes, or no.

Mr. HALL. I do not have an opinion on that, we will do whatever you like.

Mr. FERGUSON. I would suggest that we are $20 trillion in debt. I will let the answer stand for itself there. Next, can you accurately talk about how the proposed reforms, tax reform policy, the rolling back of the regulatory cost, possible trade policy changes, spending in defense, infrastructure and poverty initiations simultaneously affect the budget?

Mr. HALL. No, we would have to do a lot of specifics and do a lot more work.

Mr. FERGUSON. It just seems, you know, it is awfully tough for us to have an honest conversation if we do not accurately know where we are going with these numbers and how they are actually going to affect us. Do you think that we should be using more dynamic scoring models based on predictive analytics to give your office and those around you more tools to accurately reflect what the policy changes are going to suggest?

Mr. HALL. I think the policy right now is working well, the dynamic scoring we believe makes for a more accurate forecast. And it really makes a difference on the large pieces of legislation and that is when we are required to use it, so that seems appropriate. We are going to continue to get better at it and quicker at it but I think it does probably help improve the accuracy.

Mr. FERGUSON. You know, as we sit around and we talk about this, the [inaudible] mandatory spending and I think we are going to have to be honest with ourselves and the American people about the promises that have been made and our ability to continue to keep those promises. We are going to have tough decisions to make and it is you know, I kind of look at it and we talk about where we are in the budget process, are we going to have a budget that balances in 10 years, are we going to have one that balances in 5 years, is it going to be one that balances in 12 years.

Are we not going to vote for a balanced budget because it ruins the political purity of a particular representative? I just get the sense until we are willing to fundamentally address and honestly address the mandatory spending crisis that we are not doing anything more than rearranging the deck chairs on the Titanic. Is that a fair statement?

Mr. HALL. I want to be fair and say that there are a lot of ways you can address it, you do not have to just focus on mandatories. The broader way.

Mr. FERGUSON. Dr. Hall you said earlier, the question I might be paraphrasing, all of the mandatory spending is going to outstrip all of the discretionary spending.

Mr. HALL. That is right, and the spending is mandatory.

Mr. FERGUSON. Thank you.

Mr. HALL. That is right.

Mr. FERGUSON. So, I mean it is coming, at some point it is going to eat up every single resource we've got so we have to address that. You know, the other thing and I will close with this. You know it is interesting, I kind of feel we are a political version of Thelma and Louise right now. We have been, just in this here, and we have been talking about who has been the better driver for the last 50 miles. And now we are fussing about who is driving and the car is about to go over the cliff and it does not matter who is right or who is wrong if we do not stop that car from going over the cliff.

The American people expect us to stop this car from going over the cliff and I think it is a real challenge that we have as a Congress and as an American people to have those very honest conversations that we have got to have. We have to get better at scoring the budget, I believe we have to get better at scoring the proposed changes. I think we have to able to strip the emotion and the politics out of our decision and use better analytics to make these tough decision and with that Madam Chair I yield back.

Interim Chair BLACK. The gentleman yields back. The gentleman from Wisconsin, Mr. Grotham, is recognized for 5 minutes.

Mr. GROTHAM. Thank you. I want to take up again a little bit looking into why the economy is doing so poorly, you know this 1.6 percent growth is kind of pathetic with all of the new technology that is out there. Labor participation rate is 62.7 percent and I want talk a little bit more about these entitlements because in the last decade, means tested spending has gone up from about $670 billion to $740 billion, so more than double. When you look at so many of these programs it is like they were designed by politicians who intentionally either wanted to keep people out of the labor force or not making a lot of money.

And I want you to comment a little bit on whether, say if we did something about low income housing, where we kind of give people free housing as long as you do not work. Or the earned income tax credit where we like punish people if they make more than $19,000 a year.

Do you think we could begin to lift these numbers up, lift up the GDP as well as lift up our tax collections if we were to get rid of some of these programs and free people from the incentives not to work? I mean in my district my employers again and again I feel, "Glenn it is tough competition out there to find workers and the toughest competition is from the Federal Government that is paying people not to work for me." Could you comment on what would happen if we would scale back some of these programs?

Mr. HALL. Well, sure, obviously, we would need some specifics to actually do a real score and do it carefully. And of course, repealing some of these programs would have some other effects that you might want to consider. But we do a number of things, and we make a point of putting it out occasionally, which are implicit taxes on working that if people work more and earn more they lose benefits or if they begin to work they lose benefits. So, that is part of our calculation when we look at something we look and see what impact it has on supply of labor, willingness of people to work, and that is consideration.

Mr. GROTHAM. Could you easily come up with a hypothetical in which people, say if they work and make another $10,000, lose $10,000 in benefits between their Pell Grants and their earned income tax credit and their food stamps and low income housing.

Mr. HALL. Well I mean those are all reasonable versions of that. For example, we have been talking a little bit about the ACA, that is part of the issue about the ACA the decline in the labor supply is essentially an implicit tax on working where you lose your health benefits.

Mr. GROTHAM. And it is not just a decline on labor supply, I think a lot of these programs will encourage you to work but not very hard. You know the earned income tax credit was clearly designed to discourage somebody to make more than $20,000 a year. Right?

I mean that is what it appears it was designed to do. There are various different cliffs in the Affordable Care Act. I was in a different hearing yesterday in which an accountant talked about people holding down their income to get their subsidies. So, in other words again the Affordable Care Act was designed by somebody who wanted to discourage Americans from working hard, correct?

Mr. HALL. Well, I do not know that was the reason for it, but certainly looking at the possible side effects of programs, at what affects they may have on incentives is an important part of any public policy analysis I think.

Mr. GROTHAM. We can do both a great step towards reducing things on the spend side and getting a big increase on income collection if we paired back some of these programs and allowed people to work. When, you know, you run into people back in the district that have stories, some of you do not talk to these people but you talk to their parents, you talk to their siblings and they will tell you, you know. My brother, my sister, my daughter, they are not working because of the benefits. You think we could make a big step towards balancing the budget if we pared some of these things back?

Mr. HALL. It would undoubtedly have an impact. I do not know if it would get us towards balancing the budget because this is such a big problem. But that could have some significant impact if one looked at some of the programs and worried about the incentives.

Mr. GROTHAM. Well, means tested spending, according to what I have here, went up about $370 billion in the last 10 years, I mean that by itself would be almost half way towards balancing our budget. And you turn around and look at the huge degree in which we discourage people from working and also you get that income tax coming in. I suppose you would just be afraid to take a ballpark estimate on what would happen.

Mr. HALL. And that is right and there is an element too of a one-time change and then apart of what we are looking for is the more permanent change. What happens to not just labor supply, but the growth of the labor supply going forward.

Mr. GROTHAM. Well, thanks for coming over here its enjoyable listening to you.

Interim Chair BLACK. The gentleman's time is expired. As we conclude today, I just want to clip off a few things to help us recognize what a situation we are in as a country right now, and how desperate we are to change the current trajectory that we are on.

And so, let me just clip off a few reminders. Real GDP grew only by 1.6 percent last year, a 5 year low and half the long-term average growth rate in this U.S. Since the recession ended in 2009 the economy has grown by an average of 2.1 percent making this the weakest economic recovery of the modern era. The headline on unemployment rate has declined sharply in the recent years and currently stands at 4.7 percent and that all sounds good but the other aspects of the labor market remain weak. The broader unemployment rate, which includes those, working part-time because they cannot find full-time work and discourage workers who have stopped looking for work is 9.2 percent nearly double the headline rate.

The labor workforce participation rate, which I continue to remind people in my district as they hear the low rate that is only unemployment rate, that really is the only the rate that matters, 62.7 percent. That means that of able-bodied workers, only 62.7 percent of them are actually employed in a full-time employment. Close to a 40-year low and CBO expects this rate to continue to decline in the future. CBO maintains that the Affordable Care Act is contributing to this decline in the overall labor supply in the economy.

The average hourly earnings have increased by about 2.5 percent over the latest year, but that is well below the previous session level when earnings were growing by about 4 percent a year. Real median household income is finally on its upswing but at $56,500, is still $900 or 1.6 percent below its pre-recession peak in 2007. So, as we can see by all of its statistics and these numbers, this is affecting our economy and more importantly this is affecting the people of this country.

So, thank you Mr. Hall for appearing before us today. Please be advised that members may submit questions to be answered later in writing. Those questions and answers will be made part of the formal hearing. Any members who wish to submit questions or any extraneous materials for the record may do so within 7 days.

Mr. YARMUTH. Madam Chair, may I make just a brief comment in response to your comments?

Interim Chair BLACK. Absolutely.

Mr. YARMUTH. In listening to both sides and to Director Hall during this hearing we heard very few ideas for stimulating growth in the economy or specifics about what we would cut or how we would fix some of the mandatory spending programs.

So, I think if it would be possible maybe to have another session in the next few months to discuss the actual recommendations that are in the new publication from Director Hall and maybe get some other people in here who can talk about how we can actually grow the economy. Because I am not exactly sure we know how to do that, either side of us.

Interim Chair BLACK. Point well taken, Mr. Yarmuth. With that the committee stands adjourned.

[Whereupon, at 12:11 p.m., the committee adjourned subject to the call of the chair.]

[The following questions and responses were submitted for the record.]

Questions for the Record

To: Interim Chairman Diane Black, House Budget Committee
From: Congressman Tom McClintock
Date: February 3, 2017
RE: Hearing: "CBO Budget and Economic Outlook"

I would like Dr. Keith Hall, who testified at the House Budget Committee's February 2, 2017, hearing to please respond to the following questions for the record in writing.

1. What sort of analysis does the Congressional Budget Office regularly produce relating to appropriations bills?

2. Many appropriations bills include changes in mandatory programs (CHIMPS). Does CBO analyze the budgetary effects of these CHIMPS?

3. Does CBO estimate the one-year, five-year, and ten-year outlays for each account funded in an appropriations bill?

4. Would CBO consider making its recurring reports and analysis related to appropriations bills available to the public, as it does with other estimates?

5. CBO annually produces reports that cover appropriations for unauthorized programs. House Committee Reports are required to identify appropriations in the bill for programs that are not authorizes. However, many significant appropriations bills that are not accompanied by Committee Reports, such as CRs or Omnibus bills, do not disclose unauthorized appropriations. Is CBO able to provide estimates of unauthorized appropriations in a timely manner before House consideration of bills not accompanied by a report?

Questions for the Record

To: Keith Hall, Ph.D., Director, Congressional Budget Office
From: Congressman Todd Rokita
Date: February 3, 2017
RE: Hearing: "CBO Budget and Economic Outlook"

1. Can you tell us how the original CBO cost estimates [of the Affordable Care Act] have aligned with reality under current law?

2. In your work, do you see anything systemically errant in the way CBO is chartered or required to score major pieces of legislation?

Congressional Budget Office

MARCH 3, 2017

Answers to Questions for the Record
Following a Hearing on the
Budget and Economic Outlook for 2017 to 2027
Conducted by the House Committee on the Budget

On February 2, 2017, the House Committee on the Budget convened a hearing at which Keith Hall, Director of the Congressional Budget Office, testified about CBO's report The Budget and Economic Outlook: 2017 to 2027 *(www.cbo.gov/publication/52370). After the hearing, two Members of the Committee submitted questions for the record. This document provides CBO's answers.*

Congressman McClintock

Question. What sort of analysis does the Congressional Budget Office regularly produce relating to appropriations bills?

Answer. Section 308 of the Congressional Budget and Impoundment Control Act of 1974 requires, in part, that CBO assist the House and Senate Budget and Appropriations Committees in carrying out their responsibilities. As part of that assistance, CBO provides the Appropriations Committees with data and other information as they consider legislation and distributes detailed reports to interested parties in the Congress that display account-level detail of the budgetary effects of that proposed legislation. CBO also provides a separate tabulation of the changes in mandatory programs (CHIMPs) included in such legislation.

Furthermore, CBO frequently presents details of the budgetary effects that would result from proposed appropriation legislation in "current status" reports, which reflect the latest stage of action for each appropriations subcommittee.[1] Current status reports are first provided when legislation is reported in the House or Senate and are updated as proposals progress through the legislative process. In addition, CBO publishes a historical tabulation of supplemental appropriations.[2]

Question. Many appropriations bills include changes in mandatory programs (CHIMPS). Does CBO analyze the budgetary effects of these CHIMPS?

1. See, for example, Congressional Budget Office, "Status of Discretionary Appropriations" (accessed March 1, 2017), www.cbo.gov/publication/17129.

2. See, for example, Congressional Budget Office, "Supplemental Appropriations: 2000–Present" (accessed March 1, 2017), www.cbo.gov/publication/17129.

Answer. Yes, CBO's analyses include estimates of the budgetary effects of all provisions in appropriation legislation, including those that the agency estimates would affect mandatory programs. As part of the estimates that it distributes for appropriation legislation, CBO provides a separate tabulation of the budgetary effects of such CHIMPs for every year in the next ten years.

Question. Does CBO estimate the one-year, five-year, and ten-year outlays for each account funded in an appropriations bill?

Answer. Yes. For each regular appropriation bill that is reported, CBO estimates total outlays for each of the first four fiscal years (including the budget year) as well as a total for the fifth through tenth years. CBO provides each appropriations subcommittee with such estimates for every account in an appropriation bill, along with the amounts of budget authority provided in that bill. That information is included in the report accompanying the bill. CBO also estimates the outlay effects in the next ten years for supplemental appropriation bills considered by the House or Senate and includes those estimates in the agency's published estimates for supplemental appropriation legislation.

Question. Would CBO consider making its recurring reports and analysis related to appropriations bills available to the public, as it does with other estimates?

Answer. Most of CBO's reports and analysis related to appropriation bills are available on the agency's website. Detailed, account-level analysis is complicated to present and is currently provided only to a limited number of interested parties, but CBO is developing a plan to make that information available to the public in an accessible format.

Question. CBO annually produces reports that cover appropriations for unauthorized programs. House Committee Reports are required to identify appropriations in the bill for programs that are not authorized. However, many significant appropriations bills that are not accompanied by Committee Reports, such as CRs or Omnibus bills, do not disclose unauthorized appropriations. Is CBO able to provide estimates of unauthorized appropriations in a timely manner before House consideration of bills not accompanied by a report?

Answer. No, CBO does not have the capacity to provide information about expired authorizations before the House considers bills not accompanied by a report. But the agency does provide a comprehensive report containing that information once a year. As the Budget Act requires, CBO reports annually on all programs and activities funded for the current fiscal year whose authorizations of appropriations have expired, as well as on all programs and activities whose authorizations of appropriations will expire during the current fiscal year.[3]

Producing the report requires substantial resources, because CBO must conduct extensive research to identify the expired and expiring authorizations of appropriations encompassed by

---

3. For CBO's most current version of the report, see *Expired and Expiring Authorizations of Appropriations* (January 2017), www.cbo.gov/publication/52368.

all previously enacted legislation, including new authorizations of appropriations as well as changes to existing ones from recently enacted legislation. CBO must also identify and compare any appropriated amounts provided for the current year with the corresponding authorization of appropriations in previous legislation. Appropriation legislation sometimes provides enough detail to identify the amount of funding provided for many of the programs and activities in question, but the primary resource that CBO uses is the committee report that accompanies the bill. That report typically provides more detail than the legislative text does.

Congressman Rokita

Question. Can you tell us how the original CBO cost estimates [of the Affordable Care Act] have aligned with reality under current law?

Answer. The incremental budgetary effects of many provisions of the Affordable Care Act (ACA) are embedded in the spending for preexisting programs (Medicare, for example) and in broad categories of federal tax revenues. As a result, for such provisions, the actual results cannot be identified.

It is more feasible to assess the effects of the insurance coverage provisions because some of them can be separately identified in the budget. CBO and the staff of the Joint Committee on Taxation (JCT) currently project that the gross cost to the federal government of the ACA's insurance coverage provisions will be lower than they originally estimated when the law was passed in March 2010. For example, CBO and JCT projected at the time that the gross cost of the provisions would be $214 billion in 2019; they currently project a cost of $148 billion in 2019, a reduction of about one-third.

Technical revisions and updates to CBO's economic projections account for part of the downward revision. For example, new data show that the growth of enrollment in health insurance through the ACA's marketplaces has been slower than expected, so CBO and JCT have revised downward their estimates of subsidies for coverage through the marketplaces, particularly the estimates for the 2016–2019 period. Another revision that reduced projected federal costs was the slowdown in the overall growth of health care costs covered by private insurance and by the Medicare and Medicaid programs. Although it is unclear how much of that slowdown is attributable to the recession and its aftermath and how much is attributable to other factors, the slower growth has been sufficiently broad and persistent to persuade the agencies to significantly lower their projections of federal costs for health care.

Judicial decisions, new legislation, and administrative actions also help explain the significant changes in the projected costs of the ACA's insurance coverage provisions. For example, the Supreme Court decision that made the expansion of eligibility for Medicaid optional for states significantly reduced projected costs. As a result of such developments, assessing the accuracy of CBO and JCT's March 2010 estimate has become more difficult over time.[4]

4. For related discussion, see Congressional Budget Office, *Federal Subsidies for Health Insurance Coverage for People Under Age 65: 2016 to 2026* (March 2016), www.cbo.gov/publication/51385.

Question. In your work, do you see anything systemically errant in the way CBO is chartered or required to score major pieces of legislation?

Answer. CBO faces few major impediments to providing timely and objective cost estimates to the Congress. The most common difficulty is adhering to the time lines established for Congressional consideration of legislation. CBO generally succeeds at ensuring that its work is timely and thorough, but the pace of Congressional work often makes it hard to accomplish that goal.

CBO's ability to adhere to tight time lines depends on the complexity of the legislative proposal being analyzed, the availability of data on which to base the analysis, how easily the agency's models can be adapted to the proposal, and whether the agency is required to prepare a dynamic analysis. Working quickly is particularly difficult when legislative language continues to evolve within tight time lines and when those time lines shift unexpectedly. When such obstacles arise, CBO stays in close contact with the Budget Committees, the committees of jurisdiction, and the Congressional leadership to ensure that the Congress is getting the information that it needs about the budgetary and economic effects of legislation.

In recent years, some lawmakers have shown interest in making changes to the way CBO does its work and in enhancing the information that it provides to the Congress. For example, the agency has recently been required to assess the macroeconomic effects of some fiscal policies, and it has devoted significant effort to developing analytical tools that enable it to do so.

Others interested in reforming the federal budget process have recommended that CBO provide more cost estimates of legislation before committee markups, focus more on the fair-value costs of federal credit programs, and incorporate debt-service costs into its formal cost estimates. Such changes could be feasible, although providing more estimates before committee markups would require additional resources.

○

www.ingramcontent.com/pod-product-compliance
Lightning Source LLC
Chambersburg PA
CBHW081124180526
45170CB00008B/2998
9781546948919